Introduction

Christmas for me is a special day in the year when my family gathers to enjoy good food, laughter and to exchange gifts and hugs. As we gather together for Christmas dinner the air is filled with the wonderful aroma of a traditional dinner cooking. There are twinkling lights on the tree and our home is decorated with many of my handmade treasures. I hope this book will give you some inspiration to create treasures of your own to celebrate this wonderful time of year.

I absolutely adore designing for Christmas, whether it's a small stitched gift for a friend or something bigger, such as a festive wall hanging for my family. Combine this with the fact that I am working with my own fabric collection and suddenly the projects take on a whole new feel of Lynette Anderson. Enjoy your Christmas stitching!

Creating the projects for this book has been a lot of fun. I started with Christmas stockings but snowmen, fir trees, stars, sleigh rides and cute reindeer quickly followed. There is a useful mixture of gifts and keepsakes for you to create, including a pillow, placemats and napkins, a wall hanging, tree decorations and a lovely table centrepiece. All of the projects are easy to create, with stepped instructions and diagrams to help you. The templates can be found at the back of the book.

With a festive mix of patchwork, appliqué and stitchery the delightful projects in this book will help you create a Christmas to remember, with keepsakes you will want to bring out year after year. And my favourite project? No contest – I love them all!

General Techniques

This section describes the basic techniques you will need to make and finish off the projects in this book, from transferring designs to binding a finished quilt. Beginners should find it very useful.

Sewing and Pressing

Patchwork or pieced work requires accurate seams and maintaining an accurate ¼in (6mm) seam allowance will give the best results. For really accurate piecing sew a *bare* ¼in (6mm) seam, as this will allow for thread thickness and the tiny amount of fabric taken up when the seam is pressed.

Generally, press seams towards the darker fabric to avoid darker colours showing through lighter colours on the right side. Press joining seams in opposite directions so they will lock together nicely and create the flattest join. Press (don't iron) and be very careful with steam as this can stretch fabric.

Joining Strips

Sometimes you will need to join fabric strips together to make them long enough for borders or binding. Joining them with a diagonal seam at a 45-degree angle will make them less noticeable, as will pressing the seams open, as shown in the diagram.

Fig 1

A

B

Using templates

The project templates are given in the Template section and most will need to be enlarged to full size on a photocopier. Trace the full size template on to paper or thin card, cut it out and use it as a pattern to cut the shape from paper. Before cutting out check whether a ¼in (6mm) seam allowance is needed, which it will be if using a needle-turn appliqué technique.

Reversing templates

Templates being used for fusible web appliqué will need to be reversed (flipped). You could place a copy of the template on to a light source with the template right side down rather than up and trace it this way. You could also trace the template on to tracing paper, turn the tracing paper over and trace the template again on to paper.

Transferring designs

Designs can be transferred on to fabric in various ways. I use a light source, such as a light box, a window or a light under a glass table. Iron your fabric so it is free of creases. Place the design right side up and then the fabric right side up on top, taping it in place. Use a fine-tipped fabric marking pen or a pencil to trace the design. If the marks might show later then use an erasable marker, such as an air-erasable or water-soluble one.

STITCH IT FOR
Christmas

Lynette Anderson

D&C
David and Charles

Contents

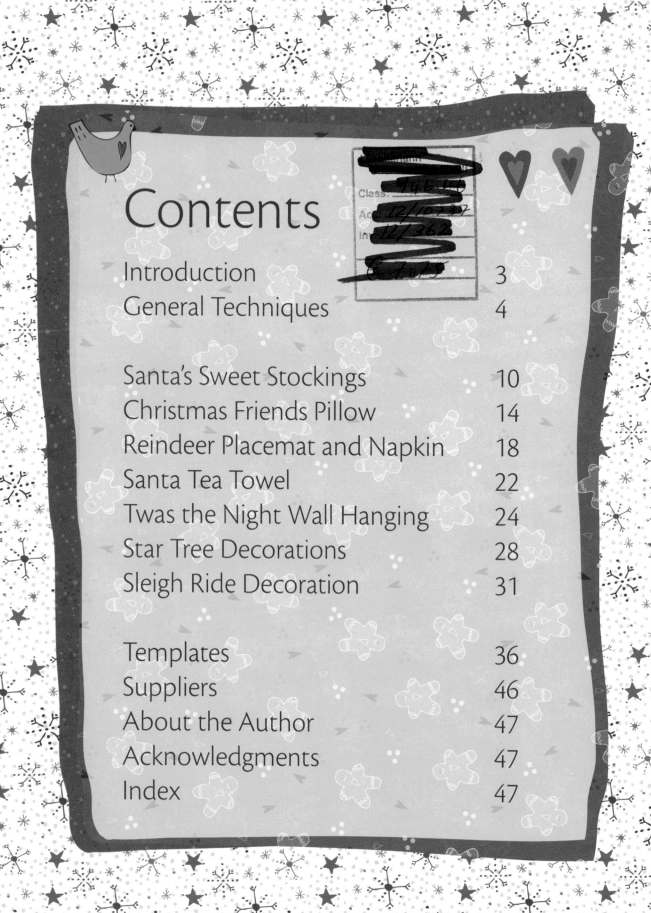

Appliqué Methods

Appliqué is the technique of fixing one fabric shape or pattern on top of another, and can be done in various ways. I have used two methods for the projects in this book – needle-turn appliqué and fusible web appliqué. You may also like to use an appliqué mat.

Needle-turn method

This is a traditional method of hand appliqué where each appliqué piece has a seam turned under all round and is stitched into position on the background fabric. The appliqué shapes may be drawn freehand or templates used, as I have done for the designs in this book.

one Mark the appliqué shape on the right side of your fabric and then mark another line further out all round for the seam allowance. This is usually ¼in (6mm) but may change depending on the size of the appliqué piece being stitched and type of fabric being used. Smaller pieces may only need a ⅛in (3mm) allowance to reduce bulk. Clip the seam allowance on concave curves (the inward ones) to make it easier to turn the seam under.

two For each appliqué piece turn the seam allowance under all round and press. Position the appliqué on the background fabric and stitch into place with tiny slip stitches all round. Press the appliqué when finished. Some people like to use the needle to turn the seam under as they stitch the appliqué in place.

Fusible web method

Fusible web has an adhesive that melts when heated so when the web is placed between two fabrics the heat of an iron causes the fabrics to fuse together, which makes it ideal for appliqué.

one When using templates for fusible web appliqué they need to be flipped or reversed because you will be drawing the shape on the back of the fabric – see Reversing Templates. Trace around each template on to the paper side of the fusible web, leaving about ½in (1.3cm) around each shape. Cut out roughly around each shape. Iron the fusible web, paper side up, on to the wrong side of the appliqué fabric and then cut out accurately on your drawn line.

two When the fusible web is cool, peel off the backing paper and place the appliqué in position on your project, right side up. (Check with the template to see which pieces need to go under other pieces, shown by dotted lines on the pattern.) Fuse the appliqué piece into place with a medium-hot iron for about ten seconds. Allow the appliqué to cool.

three The edge of the appliqué can be secured further by stitches. I normally use blanket stitch as I like the hand-crafted look but machine satin stitch can also be used.

Making a Quilt Sandwich

A quilt sandwich is a term often used to describe the three layers of a quilt – the top, the wadding (batting) and the backing.

one Press your backing fabric and hang out your wadding to reduce creases. Cut out your wadding and backing about 4in (10.2cm) larger all round than the quilt top. Prepare the quilt top by cutting off or tying in stray ends, pressing it and pressing seam allowances so they lay as flat as possible.

two Lay the backing fabric right side down on a flat surface and tape the corners to keep it flat. Put the wadding on top, smoothing out wrinkles. Now put the quilt top right side up on top.

three Secure the three layers together by using pins or safety pins, tacking (basting) or a spray glue. If using pins or tacking, use a grid pattern, spacing the lines out about 3–6in (7.6–15.2cm) apart. The sandwich is now ready for quilting.

Quilting

Quilting adds texture and interest to a quilt and secures all the layers together. I have used a combination of hand and machine quilting on the projects in this book. When starting and finishing hand or machine quilting, the starting knot and the thread end need to be hidden in the wadding (batting).

If you need to mark a quilting design on your top this can be done before or after you have made the quilt sandwich. There are many marking pens and pencils available but test them on scrap fabric first. If you are machine quilting, marking lines are more easily covered up. For hand quilting you might prefer to use a removable marker or a light-coloured pencil. Some water-erasable markers are set by the heat of an iron so take care when pressing.

Binding

Binding a quilt creates a neat and secure edge. A double-fold binding is more durable.

one Measure your completed quilt top around all edges and add about 8in (20.3cm) extra. Cut 2½in (6.3cm) wide strips and join them all together to make the length needed – see Joining Strips. Fold the binding in half along the length and press.

two Start midway along one side of the quilt and pin the binding along the edge, aligning raw edges. Stitch the binding to the quilt through all layers using a ¼in (6mm) seam until you reach a corner when you should stop ¼in (6mm) away from the end (see diagram).

Fig 2

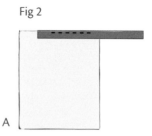

A

three Remove the work from the machine and fold the binding up, northwards, so it is aligned straight with the edge of the quilt.

B

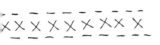

four Hold the corner and fold the binding back down, southwards, aligning it with the raw edge and with the folded corner square. Pin in position and then begin sewing again, from the top and over the fold, continuing down the next edge. Repeat with the other corners.

five When you are nearing the starting point stop 6in (15.2cm) away. Fold back the beginning and end of the binding, so they touch and mark these folds with a pin. Cut the binding ¼in (6mm) from the pin, open out the binding and join with a ¼in (6mm) seam. Press the seam open, re-fold the binding and slipstitch it in place.

six Now fold the binding over to the back of the quilt and slipstitch it in place all round. Fold the mitres at the corner neatly and secure with tiny slipstitches.

C

Embroidery stitches

I have used various stitches to create the stitcheries on the projects in this book. They are all easy to work and fun to do. Follow these simple diagrams.

Backstitch

Backstitch is an outlining stitch that I also use to 'draw' parts of the design. It is really easy to work and can follow any parts of a design you choose.

thread through to form a loop. Put your needle through the loop from front to back, making sure the loop is not twisted. As you pull the thread into place lift the stitch slightly so that it sits on top of the raw edge rather than sliding underneath it. Pull the thread firmly into place to avoid loose, floppy stitches. Continue on to make the next blanket stitch.

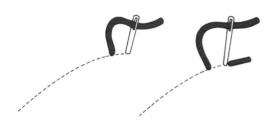

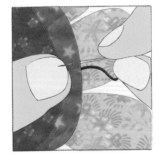

Blanket stitch

Blanket stitch is used to edge appliqué motifs. Start at the edge of the appliqué shape, taking the needle through to the back of the work and back through to the front of the shape that you are appliquéing a small distance in from the edge where you started. Pull the

7

Chain stitch

This stitch can be worked in straight or curved lines and as a single detached stitch. It can be used for flower and tree stems.

Feather stitch

Feather stitch is quite easy to form and creates an attractive pattern.

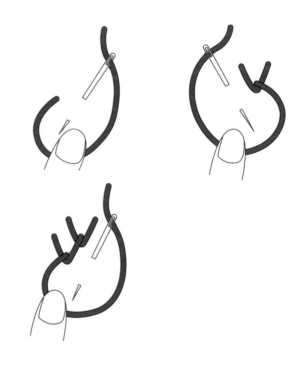

Cross stitch

A simple cross stitch can be used to add pattern to stitcheries, particularly on animal coats.

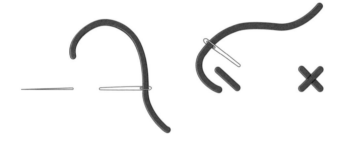

Fly stitch

This embroidery stitch is useful for creating dense lines of pattern. Single stitches can also be work as individual spot fills.

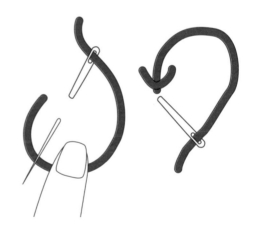

French knot

These little knots are easy to form and are useful for eyes and other details.

Running stitch

These are evenly spaced stitches that can run in any direction or pattern you choose. Quilting stitch is a running stitch.

Lazy daisy stitch

This decorative stitch is great for flowers especially if the stitches are worked in a circle.

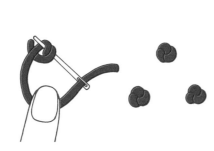

Satin stitch

This stitch is used to fill in areas of a design with long stitches worked side by side.

Long stitch

Long stitch is just a single long stitch. It is useful for stars, coat markings, cat's whiskers and so on.

Santa's Sweet Stockings

I had fun creating two different designs for these sweet Santa's stockings. Using just one thread colour the stitching is finished quite quickly making these Christmas stockings ideal for a last moment gift or decoration. See Suppliers for Mrs March fabric details.

Finished size: 7in x 9¾in (17cm x 24.8cm) approx.

What You Will Need
(for one stocking)

❄ 12in (30.5cm) square of yarn dye fabric (I used Mrs March 9021-N) for stitchery background

❄ 12in (30.5cm) square of print fabric for backing

❄ 4in (10.2cm) square each of two coordinating prints for toe and heel appliqué

❄ 5½in x 9¼in (14cm x 23.5cm) feature print for stocking cuff

❄ ¾in x 7in (2cm x 17.8cm) coordinating fabric for hanging loop

❄ 12in (30.5cm) square of stitchery stabilizer (optional)

❄ DMC stranded cotton thread: 221 country red

❄ Fine-tipped fabric marking pen

❄ Light box (optional)

❄ General sewing supplies

Transferring the Design

one Use the templates provided and enlarge to the correct size. Using a light source such as a light box or window, centre the stitchery background fabric right side up over the stitchery pattern and trace the design using a fine-tipped fabric marking pen. If using an iron-on stitchery stabilizer iron it on before starting the stitching by fusing it on to the back of your stitchery fabric. This will also help to avoid thread shadows from showing on the front of the work. Place the shiny side of the stabilizer on to the wrong side of your fabric and follow the manufacturer's instructions to bond it in place.

Making the Stocking Front

two Using the stocking pattern provided make a paper template for the toe and heel appliqué shapes – refer to General Techniques for Using Templates, Transferring Designs and also Appliqué Methods. I used the needle-turn appliqué method. Position the toe and heel pieces onto the right side of the stitchery fabric making sure they line up with the stitchery design and with the seam allowances turned under neatly. Stitch in place using a blind hem stitch.

three Now work the stitchery in red stranded cotton. The stitches used are shown on the stitcheries templates: backstitch (BS), satin stitch (SS), cross stitch (CS), running stitch (RS), feather stitch (FS), long stitch (LS) and French knots (FK). Use two strands of embroidery thread unless otherwise stated. When all the stitching has been completed, gently press your work.

four Using the template provided make a paper pattern for the stocking. With the wrong side of the stitchery front facing upwards position the template on the fabric and draw around it with a suitable fabric marking pen.

Fig 1

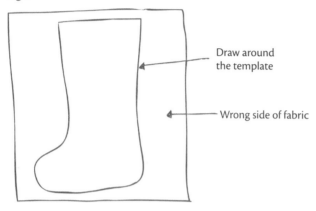

Draw around the template

Wrong side of fabric

Making the Back and Lining

five Place the embroidered stocking front and one of the print fabrics right sides together and pin to hold together. Stitch on the drawn line, leaving the top edge open. Trim, leaving ¼in (6mm) beyond the stitched line and clipping into the seams a little around the stocking curves. Turn through to the right side and press gently.

Fig 2

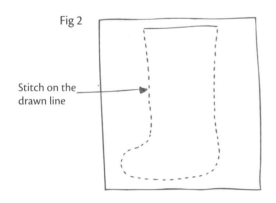

Stitch on the drawn line

Fig 3

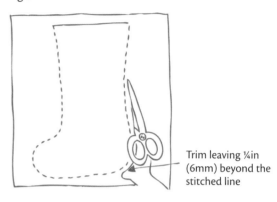

Trim leaving ¼in (6mm) beyond the stitched line

six Repeat this process with the lining pieces. Put the lining inside the outer stocking, with wrong sides together and matching the top edge and side seams. Pin the pieces together on the top edge.

Making the Cuff

seven From the feature print cut one piece 5½in x 9in (14cm x 22.9cm). Fold it in half and stitch to form a circle. Fold in half wrong sides together and press.

Fig 4

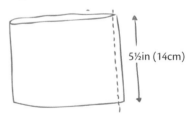

5½in (14cm)

Fig 5

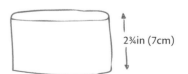

2¾in (7cm)

eight Make the hanging loop by pressing approximately ⅜in (1cm) in along both long sides of the ¾in x 7in (2cm x 17.8cm) strip. Fold in half and stitch. Fold the 7in (17.8cm) hanging loop in half and pin on the top right edge of the stocking, make sure the loop is facing down into the stocking.

Fig 6

Pin hanging loop facing inwards on seam

Right side of stocking

nine Place the stocking cuff with the folded edge facing down inside the top edge of the stocking. Pin the two raw edges together and then stitch together.

Fig 7

Place the folded cuff inside the stocking

Right side of stocking

Fig 8

Machine stitch around the top edge of the stocking

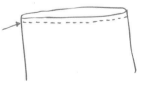

ten Turn the cuff over the edge of the stocking. As you do this the hanging loop will pop up into position. Press gently to finish.

Fig 9

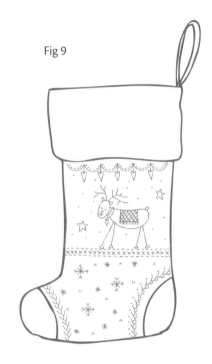

Christmas Friends Pillow

Combine blanket stitch appliqué and stitchery with some lovely fabrics and use this festive pillow to create a holiday feel for your home. Simply pieced charm squares form the background for this delightful appliquéd scene.

Finished size: 19in (48.3cm) square approx.

What You Will Need

❄ 12in (30.5cm) square of cream yarn dye fabric for appliqué background

❄ 3in x 5in (7.6cm x 12.7cm) of red snowflake print for Santa's jacket and hat

❄ 2in x 3in (5cm x 7.6cm) of cream print for Santa's face and coat trim

❄ 3in (7.6cm) square each of soft red print for snowman's scarf, and brown print for Santa's boots, belt, mittens and Snowman's hat

❄ 2½in x 3½in (6.3cm x 9cm) of soft green print for toy sack

❄ 3½in x 4½in (9cm x 11.4cm) of cream heart print for snowman

❄ 2in x 3in (5cm x 7.6cm) of white felt or wool for Santa's beard and snowflakes

❄ 5in (12.7cm) square each of nine assorted coordinating prints

❄ 4in (10.2cm) x width of fabric red star print for border

❄ 6in (15.2cm) x width of fabric red print for outer border

❄ 20in (50cm) square of fabric for backing

❄ 20in (50cm) square of muslin

❄ 20in (50cm) square of wadding (batting)

❄ DMC stranded cotton thread: 188 burnt orange, 245 country red, 312 chocolate, 367 just green, 382 beige, 925 pine green and 2500 bright white

❄ Fusible web

❄ Stuffing for pillow

Transferring the Design

one Use the templates provided and enlarge to the correct size. Using a light source such as a light box or window, centre the stitchery background fabric right side up over the stitchery pattern and trace the design using a fine-tipped fabric marking pen. If using an iron-on stitchery stabilizer iron it on before starting the stitching by fusing it on to the back of your stitchery fabric. This will also help to avoid thread shadows from showing on the front of the work. Place the shiny side of the stabilizer on to the wrong side of your fabric and follow the manufacturer's instructions to bond it in place.

Working the Appliqué and Stitchery

two You can do the appliqué now or after the stitchery has been completed. I prefer to do my appliqué before I work the stitchery. Using your favourite method of appliqué, apply the snowman, Santa and his sack on to the appliqué background fabric. I used a fusible web method of appliqué but if you decide to use needle-turn appliqué you will need to add a ¼in (6mm) seam allowance to the shapes. If using the fusible appliqué web method then reverse (flip) the templates before use. Refer to General Techniques for Making Templates and also Appliqué Methods.

three Now work the stitchery. The stitches used are: backstitch (BS), satin stitch (SS), long stitch (LS), cross stitch (CS), chain stitch (CHS), running stitch (RS), blanket stitch (BK) and French knots (FK). Use two strands unless otherwise stated. When all the stitching has been completed, gently press your work.

Key for Threads and Stitches

DMC 188 burnt orange
Snowman's nose (SS)

DMC 245 country red
Outer line (BS)
Hearts (SS)
Santa boot laces (CS and BS)
Around Santa, his hat and snowman scarf (BK)
Fringe on snowman scarf (LS)
Stars on top of trees (fill with FKs)
Crosses (X) in ground (CS)
Dots on ground (groups of three FKs)

DMC 312 chocolate
Tree trunks (CHS)
Branches and snowman stick arms (BS)
Writing and drawstring on Santa sack (BS)
Snowman and Santa eyes (FK)
Snowman buttons (SS)
Bird (BS and RS)

DMC 367 just green
Around toy bag (BK)

DMC 382 beige
Around snowman (BK)
Around Santa coat trim (BK)

DMC 925 pine green
Pine needles on trees (LS)

DMC 2500 bright white
Stars on top of snowflakes (LS)
Around Santa beard and moustache (BK)
Hill line (BS)
Dashed line under hill (RS)

four Trim the piece to within ⅜in (1cm) of the outer stitched line, creating a circle shape. Turn approximately ¼in (6mm) to the back, tack (baste) in place and press.

Fig 1

Turn under approximately ¼in (6mm) and tack(baste) in place.

Fig 2

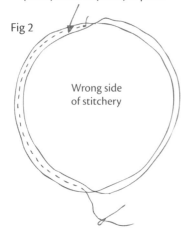

Wrong side of stitchery

Making the Pieced Pillow Front

five From the fabric chosen for the inner border (red star print) cut two pieces each 1in x 14in (2.5cm x 35.5cm) and two pieces each 1in x 15in (2.5cm x 38.1cm). From the fabric chosen for the outer border (red feature fabric) cut two pieces each 2½in x 15in (6.3cm x 38.1cm) and two pieces each 2½in x 19in (6.3cm x 48.3cm).

six Take the nine assorted 5in (12.7cm) squares of coordinating prints and join them together in three rows of three to make a 14in (35.5cm) square (including seam allowance).

Fig 3

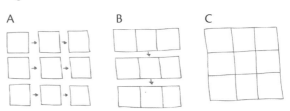

A   B   C

seven Join the inner border strips to the centre patchwork (the shorter ones first), pressing the seams outwards as you join each one on.

Fig 4

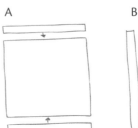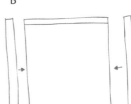

A   B

16

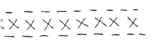

eight Now join the outer border strips to the centre square (the shorter ones first), pressing the seams outwards as you join each one on. Your square should now measure 19in (48.3cm), including seam allowance.

Fig 5

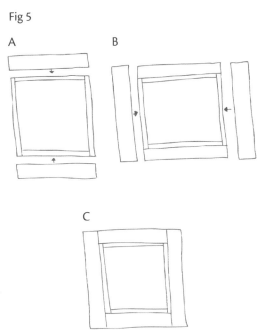

A
B
C

nine Place the patchwork right side up on a flat surface. Centre the appliqué/stitchery circle on the patchwork and when you are happy with the position pin it in place. Stitch the stitchery circle to the patchwork using a blind hem stitch. Press well and remove the tacking (basting) stitches. To remove bulk from the back carefully cut away the patchwork from behind the stitchery circle.

Fig 6

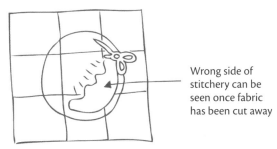

Wrong side of stitchery can be seen once fabric has been cut away

Quilting and Finishing

ten Layer the piece of muslin, the lightweight wadding (batting) and the pillow front together and quilt as desired. See General Techniques for advice on Making a Quilt Sandwich and Quilting.

eleven Place the pillow front and back right sides together and stitch around the edge with a ¼in (6mm) seam. Leave an opening of approximately 4in (10.2cm) in what will be the bottom of the pillow, to allow you to turn the pillow to the right side and fill it with stuffing. Turn the pillow through to the right side, push out the corners neatly and gently press the pillow edges. Stuff the pillow and then stitch the opening closed.

Fig 7

Place right sides together and machine stitch the two layers together

Leave open here

Reindeer Placemat and Napkin

Bring a lovely festive look to Christmas time with this fun placemat and matching napkin. They are really easy to stitch and you can make a set of six or more in no time.

Finished size: 12in x 18in (30.5cm x 45.7cm)

What You Will Need
(for one placemat and one napkin)

✳ 10in (25.4cm) square of cream heart print

✳ 10in x 19¾in (25.4cm x 50.2cm) of cream snowflake print

✳ 6in x 12½in (15.2cm x 31.8cm) of green feature print

✳ 4¾in (12cm) square of brown print for reindeer

✳ Scrap of red print for reindeer's blanket

✳ 14in x 19¾in (35.5cm x 50.2cm) of print for placemat backing

✳ 4in (10.2cm) x width of fabric red star print for placemat binding

✳ 18in (45.7cm) square of green print for napkin

✳ DMC stranded cotton thread: 221 country red, 310 black, 3781 brown and 543 off-white

✳ 14in x 19¾in (35.5cm x 50.2cm) lightweight iron-on wadding (batting)

✳ Fusible web

✳ Appliqué mat (optional)

✳ Fine-tipped fabric marking pen

✳ Light box (optional)

✳ General sewing supplies

Making the Placemat

one Cut five 4½in (11.4cm) squares from cream heart fabric, four 4½in (11.4cm) squares from cream snowflake fabric and one 6in x 12½in (15.2cm x 31.8cm) piece from green feature print.

two Using ¼in (6mm) seams, join the 4½in (11.4cm) squares together in three rows of three. Join the 6in x 12½in (15.2cm x 31.8cm) rectangle to the right side.

Fig 1

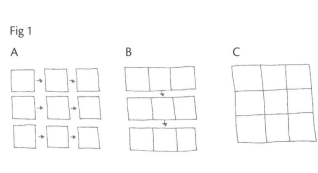

A   B   C

Fig 2

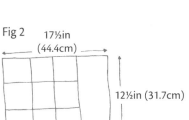

17½in (44.4cm)

12½in (31.7cm)

Working the Appliqué

three Use the templates provided to transfer the design. Using a light source such as a light box or a window, position the fabric right side up over the pattern sheet and trace the design using a fine-tipped fabric marking pen.

four I used the needle-turn method for the appliqué – see General Techniques. Remember to add a ¼in (6mm) seam allowance to the template shapes. Position the circle and reindeer pieces onto the fabric with the seam allowances turned under neatly. Stitch in place using a blind hem stitch. Now work the stitchery. The stitches used are: backstitch (BS) and satin stitch (SS). Use two strands of embroidery thread. Gently press the finished work.

Key for Threads and Stitches

DMC 221 country red

Heart (SS)

Fringe on reindeer blanket (BS)

DMC 310 black

Reindeer eyes, mouth and legs (BS)

Reindeer nose and feet (SS)

String holding heart (BS)

Stitches on reindeer blanket (BS)

DMC 3781 brown

Reindeer ears and tail (SS)

Reindeer antlers (BS)

DMC 543 off-white

Star on reindeer blanket (SS)

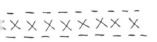

Quilting and Finishing

five Layer the backing fabric, wadding (batting) and placemat front together and quilt as desired. See General Techniques for advice on Making a Quilt Sandwich and Quilting. I chose to machine quilt my placemat with a diagonal grid pattern.

six Bind the edge of the placemat to finish using a double-fold binding – refer to Binding in the General Techniques section.

Making the Napkin

one Cut an 18in (45.7cm) square from the green print and hem it all round by machine. Using a fabric pen trace the border design on to the napkin using a light source or draw it freehand. Using two strands of DMC thread 221 country red, stitch the border using cross stitch and running stitch. This not only looks pretty but will help to hide the machine stitching on the hem.

two Cut a strip1¼in x 20in (3.2cm x 50.8cm) from red heart print for the napkin tie to finish.

Santa Tea Towel

A Christmas themed tea towel is very quick to stitch, especially if using a ready-made tea towel, and makes a great gift for friends.

Finished size: 23in x 17in (58.4cm x 43.2cm).

What You Will Need

☀ One cream ready-made tea towel about 23in x 17in (58.4cm x 43.2cm)

☀ 3in x 5in (7.6cm x 12.7cm) of red snowflake print for jacket and hat

☀ 2in x 3in (5cm x 7.6cm) of cream print for Santa face and coat trim

☀ 3in (7.6cm) square of brown print for boots, belt and mittens

☀ 2½in x 3½in (6.3cm x 9cm) of soft green print for toy sack

☀ 2in x 3in (5cm x 7.6cm) of white felt or wool for beard and moustache

☀ DMC stranded cotton thread: 245 country red, 312 chocolate, 382 beige, 925 pine green and 2500 bright white

☀ Fusible web

☀ Three tiny red heart buttons (optional)

☀ Appliqué mat (optional)

☀ Fine-tipped fabric marking pen

☀ Light box (optional)

☀ General sewing supplies

Transferring the Design

one Use the templates provided. Using a light source such as a light box or window, centre the stitchery background fabric right side up over the stitchery pattern and trace the design using a fine-tipped fabric marking pen. If using an iron-on stitchery stabilizer iron it on before starting the stitching by fusing it on to the back of your stitchery fabric. This will also help to avoid thread shadows from showing on the front of the work. Place the shiny side of the stabilizer on to the wrong side of your fabric and follow the manufacturer's instructions to bond it in place.

Working the Appliqué

two You can do the appliqué now or after the stitchery has been completed, I prefer to do my appliqué before the stitchery. Using your favourite method of appliqué, apply Santa and his sack. I used a fusible web method but if you prefer a needle-turn method you will need to add seam allowance to the shapes. Refer to General Techniques for Using Templates, Transferring Designs and Appliqué Methods.

three Now work the stitchery. The stitches used are: backstitch (BS), long stitch (LS), cross stitch (CS), chain stitch (CHS), blanket stitch (BK) and French knots (FK). Use two strands of embroidery thread. When all the stitching has been completed, gently press your work.

Binding

four Bind the edge of the tea towel to finish using a double-fold binding – see Binding in General Techniques. Stitch on three tiny red heart buttons on the tree to finish or work the hearts in red backstitch instead.

Key for Threads and Stitches

DMC 245 country red

Boot laces (CS and BS)

Around Santa and hat (BK)

Star on top of tree (fill with FKs)

DMC 312 chocolate

Tree trunks (CHS)

Branches (BS)

Writing and drawstring on sack (BS)

Santa's eyes (FK)

DMC 382 beige

Around toy bag (BK)

Around coat trim (BK)

DMC 925 pine green

Pine needles on trees (LS)

DMC 2500 bright white

Around Santa's beard and moustache (BK)

Twas the Night Wall Hanging

This festive wall hanging shows Santa all ready for his big night of the year. This sweet stitchery has a variety of stitches for you to try, including feather stitch, French knots and cross stitch. A simple log cabin border sets off the stitchery to perfection and some hand-painted buttons add a lovely finishing touch (see Suppliers).

Finished size: 11in x 13in (28cm x 33cm) approx.

What You Will Need

* 7in x 9in (17.8cm x 22.9cm) of speckled cream fabric for stitchery background (or larger if working with an embroidery hoop)

* 1½in x 12in (3.8cm x 30.5cm) each of eight assorted coordinating prints for log cabin borders

* 11in x 17in (28cm x 43.2cm) of fabric for rod pocket and backing

* 15cm (6in) x width of fabric dark green print for binding

* 12in x 14in (30.5cm x 35.5cm) wadding (batting)

* DMC stranded cotton threads: 221 country red, 310 black, 712 cream, 758 flesh, 780 mustard, 924 country blue, 931 soft blue, 935 dark green, 3022 grey, 3033 off-white and 3820 old gold

* DMC rayon thread: silver 30415

* Hand-painted buttons: one heart, one gingerbread man, one star and one moon

* Stitchery stabilizer (optional)

* Fine-tipped fabric marking pen

* Light box (optional)

* General sewing supplies

Transferring the Design

one Use the templates provided. Using a light source such as a light box or window, centre the stitchery background fabric right side up over the stitchery pattern and trace the design using a fine-tipped fabric marking pen. If using an iron-on stitchery stabilizer iron it on before starting the stitching by fusing it on to the back of your stitchery fabric. This will also help to avoid thread shadows from showing on the front of the work. Place the shiny side of the stabilizer on to the wrong side of your fabric and follow the manufacturer's instructions to bond it in place.

Working the Stitchery

two Work the stitchery using the following key. The stitches used are: backstitch (BS), cross stitch (CS), satin stitch (SS), French knots (FK) fly stitch (FYS), feather stitch (FS), running stitch (RS), chain stitch (CHS) and long stitch (LS). Use two strands of embroidery thread unless otherwise stated. When all the stitching has been completed, gently press your work on the wrong side.

Key for Threads and Stitches

DMC 221 country red
Outline of coat (BS)
Crosses (X) inside coat (CS)
Dots inside coat (FK)
Inner line around star and moon button box (BS)
Santa's mouth (BS)
Dots on feather stitch outer border (FK)

DMC 310 black
Outline of boots, gloves and belt (BS)
Shoe laces and toy bag string (BS, one strand)
Vertical lines on belt (LS)

DMC 712 cream
Outline of beard and moustache (BS)
Fill for beard and moustache (RS)

DMC 758 flesh
Outline of face (BS)

DMC 780 mustard
Dots inside both stars (FK)
Heart belt buckle (SS)
Dots around star and moon button box (FK)

DMC 924 country blue
Box outline around gingerbread man button (RS and CS)

Outline of toy bag (BS)
Alternate lines inside toy bag (BS)
Dashed line around star and heart box (RS)
Crosses (X) around star and moon box (CS)

DMC 931 soft blue
Santa's eyes (FK)

DMC 935 dark green
Tree trunk (CHS)
Tree branches (FS)
Outer border (FS)
Crosses (X) around star and heart button box (CS)

DMC 3022 grey
Alternate lines inside toy bag (BS)

DMC 3033 off-white
Outline trim on coat, hat and pom-pom (BS)
Fur trim on coat (fill with FKs)

DMC 3820 old gold
Outline star on top of tree and in box (BS)
Sparks coming from star on top of tree (BS)

DMC Rayon 30415
Snowflakes (FYS, one strand)
Dots on snowflakes (FK)

Making the Log Cabin Borders

three Trim the stitchery down to 7in x 9in (17.8cm x 22.9cm), including seam allowance. Take the 1½in (3.8cm) wide assorted strips and decide which order you want them to be used as the borders for the stitchery. Now cut the eight strips to the correct lengths, as follows (see diagram).

1) One strip 1½in x 9in (3.8cm x 22.9cm).
2) One strip 1½in x 8in (3.8cm x 20.3cm).
3) One strip 1½in x 10in (3.8cm x 25.4cm).
4) One strip 1½in x 9in (3.8cm x 22.9cm).
5) One strip 1½in x 11in (3.8cm x 28cm).
6) One strip 1½in x 10in (3.8cm x 24.5cm).
7) One strip 1½in x 12in (3.8cm x 30.5cm).
8) One strip 1½in x 11in (3.8cm x 28cm).

four Take the 12in x 14in (30.5cm x 35.5cm) piece of wadding (batting) and centre the stitchery right side up on top of the wadding. Using the diagram as a guide and using ¼in (6mm) seams, add the eight strips to the centre stitched piece in the order shown in the diagram, stitching through the wadding. Press each strip outwards as you go. Once all the log cabin strips have been added, the patchwork should measure 11in x 13in (28cm x 33cm).

Fig 1

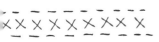

Making the Rod Pocket and Backing

five Cut an 11in x 13in (28cm x 33cm) piece of fabric for the backing and a 1in x 4in (2.5cm x 10.2cm) strip for the rod pocket. Take the strip for the rod pocket and press approximately ¼in (6mm) in on each end. Press another ¼in (6mm) and then stitch in place. Fold the rod pocket in half lengthwise (raw edges together) and press. Now machine stitch the rod pocket to the top edge of the backing fabric.

Fig 2

Fig 3

2in (5cm)

Binding

six On a flat surface place the backing right side down and place the quilted front on top so wrong sides are together and pin together. Bind the wall hanging – see Binding in General Techniques. Remove the pins and stitch the buttons in place to finish.

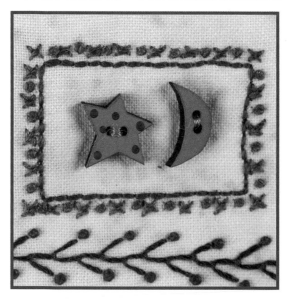

Star Tree Decorations

It's always nice to add to your supply of tree decorations, especially if they are as pretty as these little stars. I have created three designs, each made with some simple fusible web appliqué and easy embroidery stitches. Using a variety of green and red prints will make the star display more interesting.

Finished size: 3¾in x 3¾in (9.5cm x 9.5cm) approx.

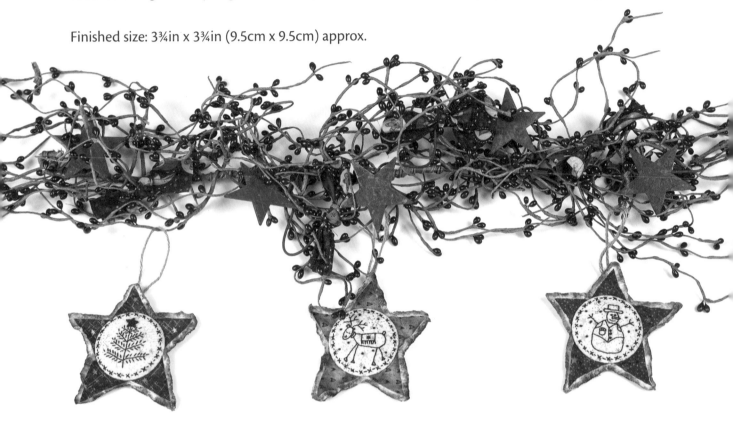

What You Will Need
(for one star)

❄ 5in x 10in (12.7cm x 25.4cm) of red or green print

❄ 5in (12.7cm) square of cream snowflake print

❄ 12in (30.5cm) length of twine for tie

❄ 5in (12.7cm) square of cotton wadding (batting)

❄ 5in x 10in (12.7cm x 25.4cm) of fusible web

❄ Fabric stiffener

❄ 2in (5cm) diameter of plastic dome to mount stitchery

❄ DMC stranded cotton thread: 221 country red

❄ Instant coffee

❄ Old paintbrush

❄ Fine-tipped fabric marking pen

❄ Light box (optional)

Transferring the Design

one Use the templates provided. Using a light source such as a light box or a window, position the stitchery background fabric right side up over the stitchery pattern of your choice and trace the design using a fine-tipped fabric marking pen (I used a brown Zig Millennium).

Working the Stitchery

two Work the stitchery using two strands of red embroidery thread. The stitches used are: backstitch (BS), French knots (FK), running stitch (RS) and cross stitch (CS) and are identified on the patterns in the Template section. When all stitching has been completed, gently press your work on the wrong side.

three Cut out the fabric on the outside circular line. Work a row of running stitches around the edge of the circle, approximately ⅛in (3mm) in from the edge, using a double strand of sewing thread. Place the plastic dome on to the wrong side of the stitched circle and gently pull on the running stitches to gather the circle tightly around the plastic dome. Finish off the thread securely.

Preparing the Star

four Take the red print and trace two stars onto the fusible web. Fuse one star on to the cotton wadding (batting). Cut the star out leaving about ⅛in–¼in (3mm–6mm) of wadding showing around the star. Cut out another star, take the second red print star and centre it on the back of the wadding star and fuse in place. Dampen the star and squeeze out the excess water – this will give your star a scrunched look. Mix up a small amount of strong instant coffee and use a paintbrush to paint around the edges and sides of the wadding to give the star a nice aged look.

five Now stiffen the star using fabric stiffener, following the manufacturer's instructions for use. Leave the star to dry – it should be very stiff once dry.

six Stitch the covered dome to the stiffened star. Stitch the twine tie in place at the top of the star to finish.

Sleigh Ride Decoration

What a wonderful decoration this is, with happy reindeer waiting patiently in line munching on mistletoe while Santa delivers his surprises. Appliqué, stitchery, buttons and bells combine to make this a favourite piece you can use to decorate a table or sideboard.

Finished size: 20in (51cm) diameter approx.

What You Will Need

- 21in (53.3cm) width of fabric red star print for scalloped border and backing
- One fat quarter of yarn dye fabric for appliqué/stitchery background (I used Mrs March 9021-N – see Suppliers)
- 5in (12.7cm) square of red snowflake print for centre
- 5in (12.7cm) square each of two chocolate brown prints for reindeer
- 5in (12.7cm) square of red heart print for sleigh
- 5in (12.7cm) square of green print for Santa's sack
- Scrap of cream print for stocking cuff
- DMC stranded cotton threads: 310 black, 221 country red, 3011 green, 3781 brown and ecru
- Four tiny bells (I used gold ones but red or green would also look great)
- Two hand-painted Lynette Anderson red polka dot star buttons (see Suppliers)
- Stitchery stabilizer (optional)
- 13¾in (35cm) square of lightweight iron-on wadding (batting)
- Light box (optional)
- Fine-tipped fabric marking pen
- Roxanne's Glue Baste It ™ (optional)

Transferring the Design

one Use the templates provided and enlarge to the correct size. Copy the three patterns and join them together to form the complete design (see first diagram). Fold your stitchery background fabric into four and lightly press the folds – this will help you to centre the design on the background fabric. Open out the folded fabric and using a light source, such as a light box or window, centre the fabric right side up over the pattern and use a fine-tipped fabric marking pen to carefully trace all the stitchery lines.

Working the Appliqué

two Using your favourite method of appliqué, prepare all the shapes (reindeer head and body, blanket, sleigh, toy bag, stocking cuff and centre circle). If using a fusible web method of appliqué use the templates the size they are after enlargement and then reverse (flip) them. If using needle-turn appliqué, as I did, add seam allowances to the shapes. For the needle-turn appliqué, I made templates for the appliqué shapes from paper. Refer to General Techniques for Using Templates and Appliqué Methods.

three When your needle-turn appliqué shapes are prepared use the picture as a guide to position the shapes. To make this job easier I used a light box, placing the pattern sheet onto the light box and positioning the background fabric on top. You can usually see through the fabric well enough to position the appliqué shapes. Once you are happy with the positions glue baste or pin the shapes in place. When using traditional appliqué, I use Roxanne's Glue Baste It ™ to fix the shapes on the background. This has a small tube through which tiny drops of glue emerge, allowing for fine placement of the glue. You could use pins but I find that thread gets caught around pins when I'm sewing the shapes.

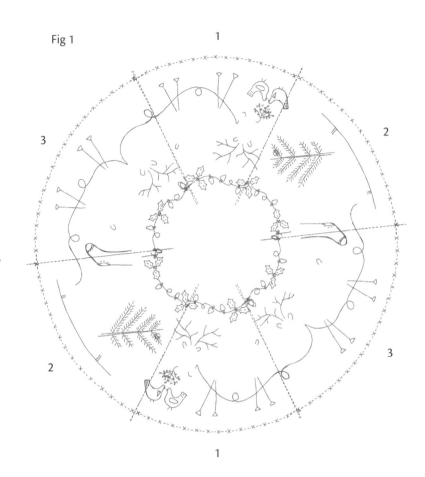

Fig 1

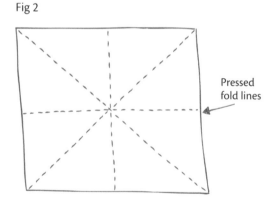

Fig 2

Pressed fold lines

four Stitch the appliqué shapes into position using a blind hem stitch and matching thread.

Working the Stitchery

five If using iron-on stitchery stabilizer fuse it to the back of your stitchery fabric before starting the stitching.

six Now work the stitchery. The stitches used are: backstitch (BS), satin stitch (SS), cross stitch (CS), running stitch (RS), lazy daisy (LD), long stitch (LS) and French knots (FK). Use two strands unless otherwise stated. Gently press your completed work.

Key for Threads and Stitches

DMC 221 country red
Reindeer collars (SS)
Holly berries (FK, six strands)
Random light bulbs (SS)
Heart on dove chests (SS)
Stocking (BS)
Line on top of stocking (BS and CS)
Dashed line on outer border (RS)

DMC 310 black
Reindeer eyes, mouths and legs (BS)
Reindeer noses and feet (SS)
Dove eyes (FK, one strand)
Dove beaks (SS)
Dove legs (BS)
String for light bulb garland (BS)
String holding stockings (BS)
Drawstring and tie on toy sack (BS)
Writing 'Toys' (BS)
Runners on sleigh (BS)

DMC 3011 green
Holly leaves (BS)
Veins on holly leaves (RS)
Pine needles on tree (LS)
Random light bulbs (SS)
Crosses (X) in outer border (CS)
Mistletoe in reindeer mouths (BS)
Leaves on mistletoe (LD)

DMC 3781 brown
Reindeer ears and tails (SS)
Reindeer antlers (BS)
Tree trunk and branches (BS)
Doves (BS)

Ecru
Mistletoe berries (FK)
Stars on reindeer blankets (SS)
Random light bulbs (SS)
Fringe on two reindeer blankets (LS)

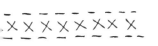

Making the Scalloped-Edge Backing

seven Cut the red star print in half to create two pieces each approximately 21¾in x 22in (55.3cm x 55.9cm). Take one of the pieces and fold it into eighths as shown in the diagram. Press firmly to create creases. These will help you position the scallop template.

Fig 3

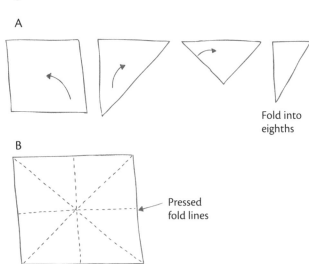

A

Fold into eighths

B

Pressed fold lines

eight Cut out the template for the scalloped edge from paper. Working on a flat surface and with the wrong side of the red star print facing upwards place the paper template on one of the eighth segments, taking care to make sure the point is in the centre and that the edges of the template line up with the creased lines you made earlier. Using a suitable fabric marking pen, draw around the scalloped top edge. Flip/reverse the template and position it in the next eighth segment and draw around the scalloped top edge again. Move to the next segment and continue in this way until all segments have been drawn.

Fig 4

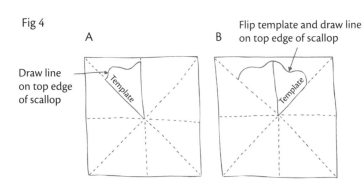

A

Draw line on top edge of scallop

B

Flip template and draw line on top edge of scallop

nine Press the folds out of the red star print. Bond the lightweight iron-on wadding (batting) on to the wrong side of the second piece of red star print.Place both red star print pieces right sides together, keeping the piece with the drawn line facing upwards. Pin the two layers together to prevent movement. Join the two pieces together by machine stitching on your drawn lines around the entire scalloped shape. Cut out approximately ¼in (6mm) beyond the stitched line.

Fig 5

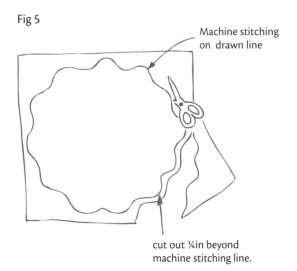

Machine stitching on drawn line

cut out ¼in beyond machine stitching line.

33

ten Clip the seam allowance to help the curves lie flat when you turn the piece to the right side. Carefully cut a short slit approximately 4in (10.2cm) in length through one layer of the red star print and pull the piece through the opening to turn it right side out. Wriggle the scallops so they sit nicely and then press.

Quilting and Finishing

eleven Centre the stitchery/appliqué on top of the scalloped backing to cover the slit and pin it in place. Stitch into position using a blind hem stitch and matching thread all around the edge.

twelve I machine quilted to hold the layers together. First, I quilted in the ditch around the centre red circle and then around the appliqué/stitchery circle. To add the finishing touches I added a row of machine stitching about ¼in (6mm) in from the scalloped edge. Finally, stitch the star buttons in place at the top of the trees and the bells on to the reindeer collars.

Fig 6

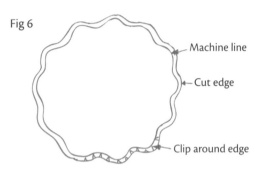

Machine line

Cut edge

Clip around edge

Fig 7

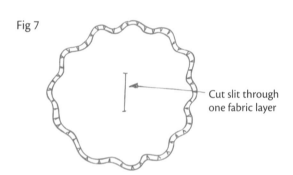

Cut slit through one fabric layer

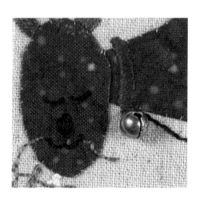

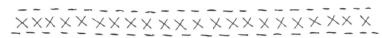

This charming decoration with its warm and welcoming colours would look wonderful as the centrepiece on the Christmas table, or be perfect to adorn a dresser or sideboard. You can also use the patterns in the book to create other projects, such as framed pictures.

35

Templates

This section contains the stitchery and appliqué templates for the projects. Most templates have had to be reduced to fit the page so please read the instructions with each template carefully. Templates being used for needle-turn appliqué will need to have seam allowances added. Templates being used for fusible web appliqué will need to be reversed (flipped). See also Using Templates, Reversing Templates and Transferring Designs.

Stitchery Templates
Enlarge by 200% to full size

Stitches Key
Backstitch (BS)   Feather stitch (FS)
Satin stitch (SS)   Long stitch (LS)
Cross stitch (CS)   French knot (FK)
Running stitch (RS)

Santa's Sweet Stockings
Appliqué Templates
Enlarge by 200% to full size

Stocking Pattern
Add seam allowance

Heel
Add seam allowance

Heel and Toe Appliqués

Toe
Add seam allowance

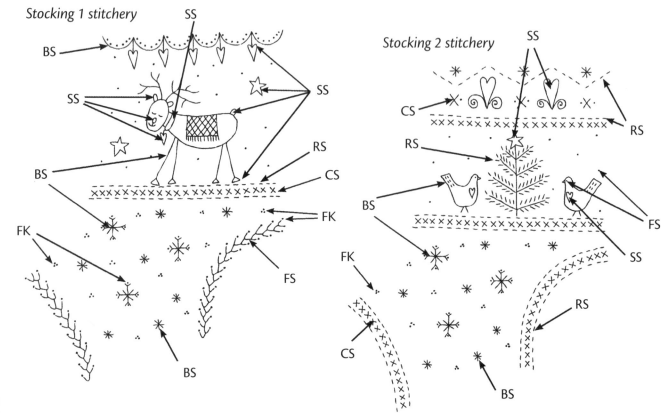

Stocking 1 stitchery

Stocking 2 stitchery

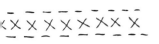

Santa's Sweet Stockings

Templates

Enlarge by 200% to full size

Christmas Friends Pillow

Templates

Enlarge by 200% to full size
Reverse (flip) the templates if using
fusible web appliqué

Red lines indicate appliqué
Blue lines indicate stitchery lines
Green lines indicate surface stitchery

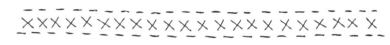

Background Circle

Reindeer Placemat

Appliqué Templates
Full size
Add ¼in (6mm) seam allowance to the shapes if using a needle turn appliqué method

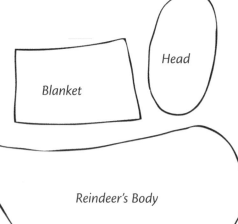

Blanket

Head

Reindeer's Body

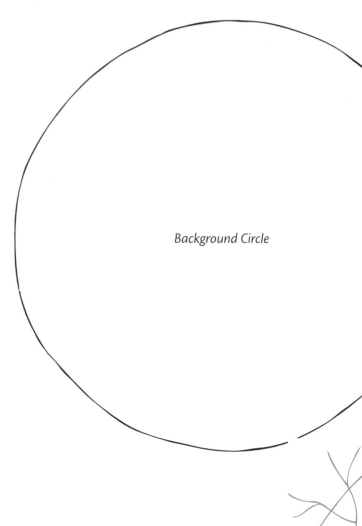

Reindeer Placemat

Stitchery Template
Full size
Red lines indicate appliqué
Blue lines indicate stitchery
Green lines indicate surface stitchery

Napkin

Border stitchery Template
Full size

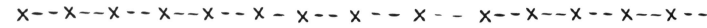

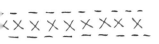

Santa Tea Towel

Appliqué Templates

Enlarge by 200% to full size
Dashed lines indicate where one
appliqué piece fits under another

Add a ¼in (6mm) seam allowance if
using a needle turn appliqué method

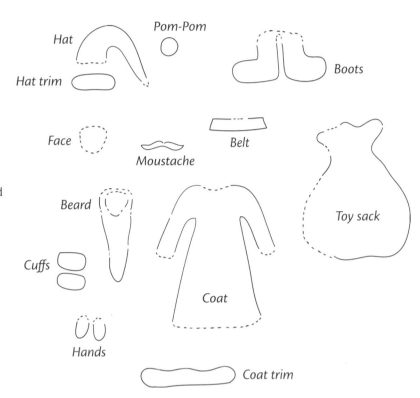

Hat

Pom-Pom

Hat trim

Boots

Face

Moustache

Belt

Beard

Cuffs

Toy sack

Hands

Coat

Coat trim

Santa Tea Towel

Stitchery Template

Enlarge by 200% to full size

Red lines indicate appliqué
Blue lines indicate stitchery
Green lines indicate surface stitchery

You could work the little hearts in red backstitch
or sew on three tiny heart buttons instead

Twas the Night Wall Hanging

Stitchery Template
Full size

Star Decorations

Template for star shape
Full size

Stitchery Template
Full size

Stitches Key
Cross stitch (CS)
Running stitch (RS)
French knot (FK)
Backstitch (BS)

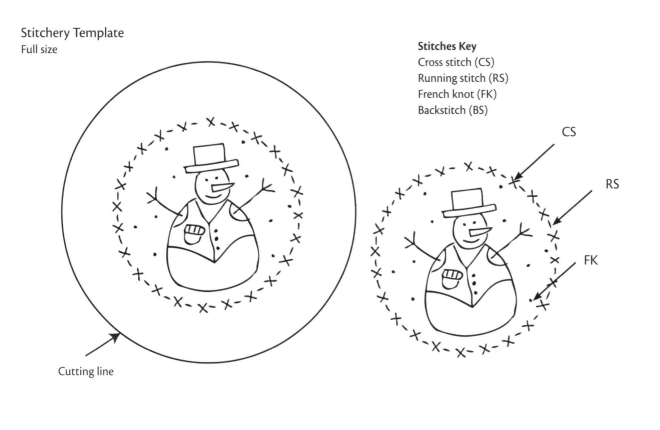

Cutting line

CS

RS

FK

Star Decorations

Stitchery Templates
Full size

Stitches Key
Cross stitch (CS)
Running stitch (RS)
French knot (FK)
Backstitch (BS)

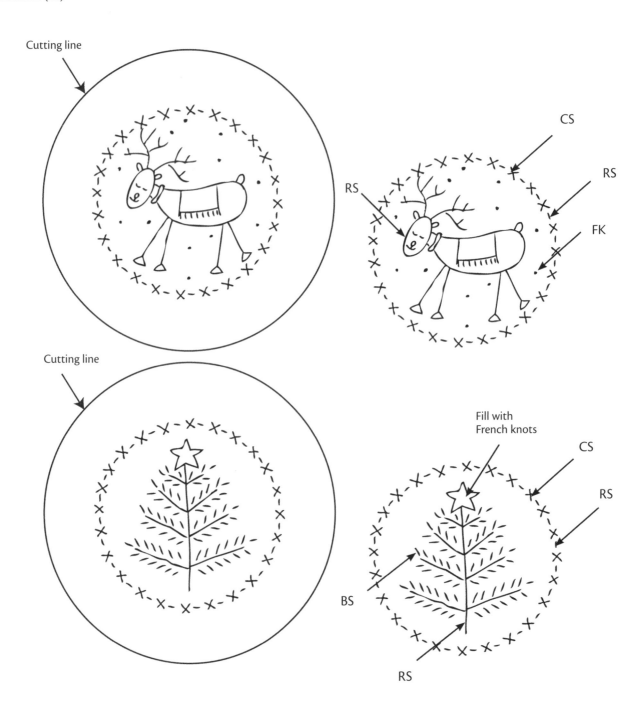

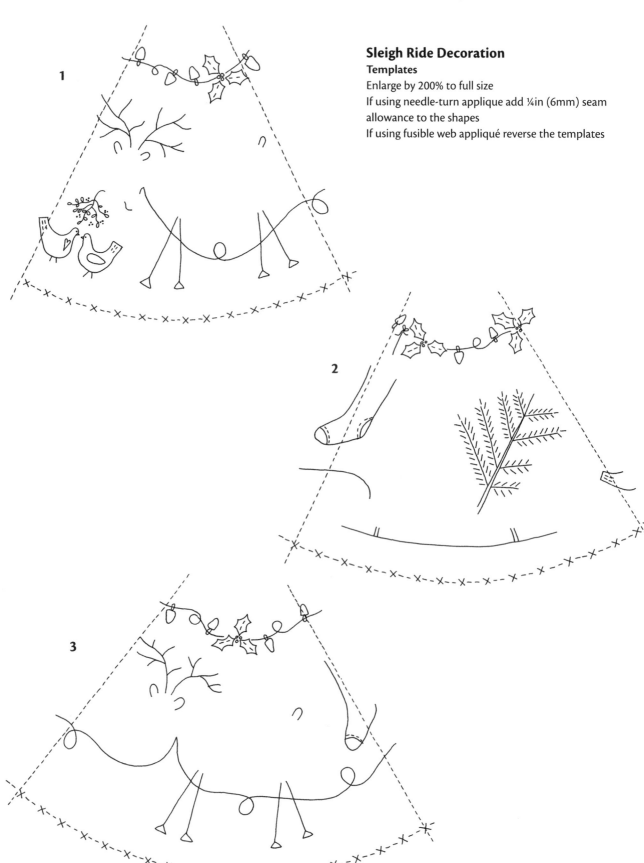

Sleigh Ride Decoration
Templates
Enlarge by 200% to full size
If using needle-turn applique add ¼in (6mm) seam
allowance to the shapes
If using fusible web appliqué reverse the templates

Sleigh Ride Decoration

Templates

Enlarge by 200% to full size

If using needle-turn applique add ¼in (6mm) seam allowance to the shapes

If using fusible web appliqué the templates need to be reversed

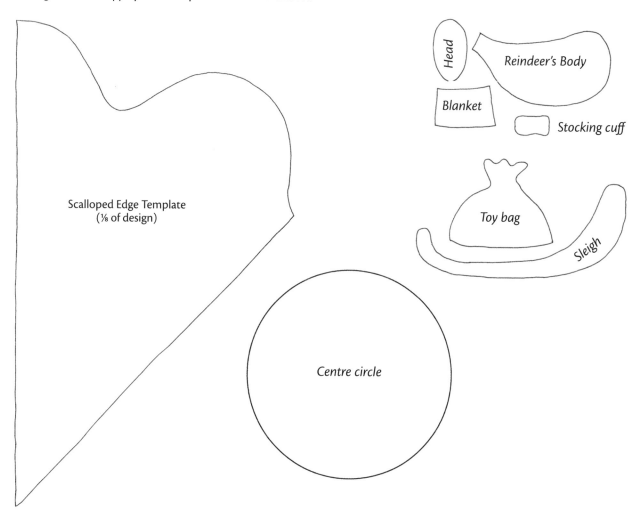

Scalloped Edge Template
(⅛ of design)

Head

Reindeer's Body

Blanket

Stocking cuff

Toy bag

Sleigh

Centre circle

Use these drawings as a guide for positioning the
appliqué shapes and working the stitchery

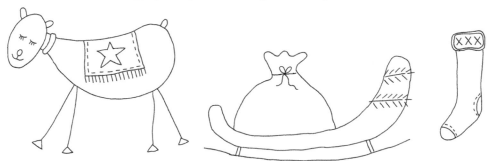

Suppliers

Lynette Anderson Designs
PO Box 9314, Pacific Paradise, QLD 4564, Australia
Tel: 07 5450 7497; from outside Australia +61 7 5450 7497
www.lynetteandersondesigns.com.au for wholesale
enquires regarding Lynette's patterns and books
www.lynetteandersondesigns.bigcartel.com for hand-
painted wooden buttons
Blog: www.lynetteandersondesigns.typepad.com
Twitter: @lynettestitches

Classic Country Living
48 Maple Street, Maleny, QLD Australia
Tel: 07 5499 9005

DMC Creative World Ltd
1st Floor Compass Building, Feldspar Close, Enderby,
Leicestershire LE19 4SD, UK
Tel: 0116 275 4000
Fax: 0116 275 4020
www.dmccreative.co.uk
*For embroidery fabrics, stranded cotton, metallic threads
and other embroidery supplies*
*Fabrics from Lecien's Mrs March collection were used for the
yarn dye fabrics*

Lecien Fabrics
5515 Doyle Street, Suite 6, Emeryville, CA 94608, USA
Tel: +1 510 596 3085
Fax: + 1 510 596 3004
Email: info@lecienusa.com
www.lecienusa.com
For fabrics, including those designed by Lynette Anderson

Sandra Faye Photographer
www.sandrafayephotographer.com.au

About the Author

Lynette Anderson's love affair with textiles began at a young age when her grandmother taught her to embroider and knit. Patchwork caught Lynette's attention in 1981 after the birth of her first son, and her affinity with textiles is apparent in her work. Moving with her family to Australia in 1990 prompted the release of Lynette first patterns in 1995 and during the ensuing years Lynette has produced hundreds of patterns. Lynette's distinctive, yet sophisticated naïve design style encompasses quilts, pillow, bags and sewing accessories. Her popular self-published books include, *Bearly Stitched*, *Sunflower Stitching*, *An Angel's Wish*, *Friends For Christmas* and *Rainbow Cottage*. Lynette was very excited when she was asked to design fabric for Lecien with whom she launched her first line 'Summertime Friends' in 2010 with 'Scandinavian Christmas' and 'Secret Garden' following in 2011. Lynette's first book for David & Charles, *It's Quilting Cats & Dogs*, was published in 2010, followed by *Country Cottage Quilting* in 2012. Visit Lynette at www.lynetteandersondesigns.typepad.com

Acknowledgments

Thank you to all the wonderful people in my life, particularly my husband Vince and my mum and dad, without whom I would not have had the energy to stitch like crazy to complete the projects for this book. A big thank you to Val Tanner, even though you tell me that your 'eyes are not so good these days' your stitching is so neat and I love working with you x. Thank you also to Helen for the loan of the vintage furniture.

Index

A DAVID & CHARLES BOOK
© F&W Media International, Ltd 2012

David & Charles is an imprint of F&W Media International, Ltd
Brunel House, Forde Close, Newton Abbot, TQ12 4PU, UK

F&W Media International, Ltd is a subsidiary of F+W Media, Inc
10151 Carver Road, Cincinnati OH45242, USA

Text and Designs © Lynette Anderson 2012
Layout and Photography © F&W Media International, Ltd 2012

First published in the UK and USA in 2012

A catalogue record for this book is available from the British Library.

ISBN-13: 978-1-4463-0253-8 paperback
ISBN-10: 1-4463-0253-9 paperback

Paperback edition printed in China by RR Donnelley for:
F&W Media International, Ltd
Brunel House, Forde Close, Newton Abbot, TQ12 4PU, UK

10 9 8 7 6 5 4 3 2 1

Acquisitions Editor: Sarah Callard
Editor: James Brooks
Project Editor: Lin Clements
Art Editor: Jodie Lystor
Photographer: Sandra Faye
Senior Production Controller: Kelly Smith

F+W Media publishes high quality books on a wide range of subjects.
For more great book ideas visit: **www.rucraft.co.uk**

Pupil Book 6C

Series Editor: Peter Clarke

Authors: Jeanette Mumford, Sandra Roberts, Andrew Edmondson

Contents

Think it through

Solve multi-step problems, and problems involving fractions, decimals and percentages

1 At the flower shop a bunch of tulips costs 99p and roses cost 50p each.

   a Lisa buys 4 bunches of tulips. How much does she spend?

   b John has £5 to spend on roses. How many can he buy?

   c Gavin buys 2 bunches of tulips and 2 roses. How much does he spend?

2 1480 people go to the school fair.

   a If everyone pays 60p to get in, how much was taken?

   b Coffee is sold for 40p a cup. 200 cups were sold. How much was spent on coffee?

   c 50% of the people that came were children. How many children came?

Work out the problems. Show your working out. If you use a calculator, write down your calculation.

1 The decorator charges £18 an hour. Paint is £4.95 a tin.

   a He has given an estimate of £171.90. This includes two tins of paint. How long does he think the painting will take?

   b One week he earns £630 for his work. How many hours did he work?

   c To paint a whole house he estimates it will need 7 tins of paint and 26 hours work. How much will it cost?

2 The post person delivered 1800 letters today.

    a 30% of the letters were first class letters. How many letters is this?

    b 5% of the letters needed signing for. How many letters is this?

    c 25% were postcards. How many is this?

3 Batteries come in packs of 2 or 4. A pack of 2 costs 95p, a pack of 4 costs £1.70.

    a Tim and Jack bought a pack of 4 and shared them. How much did they each pay?

    b Helen buys 2 packs of 2 batteries and Mark buys 1 pack of 4 batteries. How much more does Helen pay?

    c Rebecca buys 10 packs of 4 batteries. How much does she spend?

4 **a** Julia buys 4 bags of crisps. She pays with a £2 coin and gets 60p change. How much is one bag of crisps?

    b Tom buys 10 bags of crisps. How much does it cost?

    c I have £1.75 to spend. How many bags of crisps can I buy?

Five girls are competing in the long jump. Sarah jumped 5 cm further than Louise and 8 cm further than Kate. Zoe jumped $\frac{1}{10}$ m further than Louise and 40 cm further than her best friend, Rachel.

If Kate jumped 2·52 m, how far did the other girls jump?

Decimal order

 Order the decimals from smallest to largest.

a	3·4	3·45	3·5	3·54	3·55	3·44
b	7·2	7·26	7·27	7·19	7·3	7·62
c	9·11	9·19	9·1	9·2	9·28	9·18
d	4·68	4·86	4·9	4·8	4·18	4·92
e	1·71	1·07	1·7	1·17	1·77	1·75
f	2·5	2·58	2·73	2·8	2·49	2·1
g	5·8	5·64	5·18	5·1	5·46	5·49
h	12·9	12·84	12·62	12·8	12·2	12·48
i	24·7	24·5	24·75	24·93	24·17	24·9
j	48·05	48·5	48·55	48·25	48·2	48·3
k	33·82	33·28	33·8	33·03	33·3	33·6
l	18·9	18·29	18·09	18·2	18·92	18·02
m	71·6	71·86	71·8	71·48	71·4	71·06
n	48·29	48·73	48·6	48·1	48·99	48·72
o	36·03	36·82	36·1	36·9	36·72	36·3

 1 Order the decimals from smallest to largest.

a	3·2	3·26	3·02	3·254	3·367	3·102
b	5·95	5·903	5·9	5·921	5·2	5·59
c	7·426	7·406	7·4	7·41	7·004	7·04
d	8·183	8·1	8·83	8·103	8·11	8·8
e	1·7	1·75	1·755	1·577	1·57	1·55
f	2·88	2·841	2·14	2·8	2·889	2·1

g 9·006   9·06   9·66   9·69   9·669   9·6

h 0·4   0·456   0·56   0·402   0·004   0·04

i 0·22   0·225   0·2   0·26   0·226   0·62

j 1.8   1·88   1·888   1·808   1·899   1·98

2 What decimals come between these numbers?

a 12·6   and   12·61

b 30·54   and   30·548

c 24·6   and   24·609

d 72·99   and   73·001

e 15·47   and   15·479

f 62·01   and   62·1

g 54·81   and   54·817

h 38·421   and   38·43

i 14·991   and   15·005

j 29·04   and   29·17

Example

0·83

a 3·27   4·1

Copy out the numbers and arrows. Label each arrow
with the difference between the numbers.

a 3·27   4·1   5·695   6·7   7·01   8

b 1·5   1·963   2·37   4·4   5·18   6

c 2·102   2·9   3·54   4·77   5·6   7

d 5·88   6·1   7·482   8·3   8·66   9

e 4·2   4·596   5·3   6·48   7·03   8

Decimal battleships

 1 Round these decimals to the nearest whole number.

a	7·23	f	6·84
b	6·39	g	3·22
c	4·12	h	7·49
d	9·02	i	8·61
e	7·85	j	5·01

2 Round these decimals to the nearest tenth.

a	2·38	f	6·33
b	1·09	g	4·91
c	5·69	h	1·99
d	2·51	i	3·82
e	7·49	j	7·61

Decimal battleships

Play the game in the ⬤ section with these changes:

Write numbers with one decimal place between 0 and 10 in the grid, for example, 5·8.

Call out whole numbers between 0 and 10. If the number your partner calls out is the closest whole number to one of your numbers, put a line through that number. You can only cross out one number each time.

Decimal battleships

A game for 2 players

● Both players copy the grid on the right.

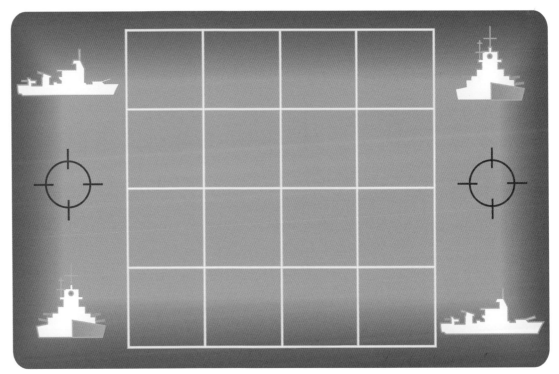

● Write a number between 5 and 10 with two decimal places in each space, for example, 6·49. Don't let your partner see your numbers.

● Choose 4 of your numbers and put a circle around them. These are your bonus numbers.

● Take it in turns to call out a number with one decimal place, for example 9·3. If the number your partner calls out is the closest tenth to one of your numbers, then you must put a line through that number. You can only cross out one number each time.

● Write down all the numbers you call out.
  Stop when you have both called out 20 numbers.

● Count how many of your numbers have not been crossed out. Any bonus numbers not crossed out are counted as two.

● The player with the highest score is the winner.

Round these numbers to the nearest tenth.

a 7·235	c 7·465	e 4·025	g 6·738	i 9·834
b 6·342	d 3·001	f 8·409	h 2·951	j 1·499

Example

6·314 → 6·3

Vertical decimals

 1 Write the number that goes with each decimal to equal 1

a 0·4	d 0·7	g 0·5
b 0·6	e 0·9	h 0·3
c 0·1	f 0·2	i 0·8

2 Write out each calculation vertically and work out the answer.

Example

$$
\begin{array}{r}
27\cdot186 \\
+\ 38\cdot503 \\
\hline
65\cdot689 \\
\hline
1
\end{array}
$$

Remember

● Align the decimal points correctly.

● Make an estimate of the answer first.

a 5·87 + 36·84	j 75·2 + 504·4
b 96·61 + 19·55	k 2·581 + 85·374
c 73·47 + 26·61	l 44·921 + 2·847
d 85.12 + 48·33	m 41·951 + 84·267
e 81·29 + 28·32	n 2·305 + 43·617
f 157·6 + 81·7	o 92.364 + 5·311
g 395·7 + 42·1	
h 347·6 + 83·7	
i 48·7 + 211·3	

1 Write out each calculation vertically and work out the answer.

a 38·48 + 51·957 + 3·54

b 7·548 + 36·45 + 7259·4

c 721·8 + 36·842 + 3·874

d 2631·7 + 6·485 + 1·36

e 423·84 + 3·801 + 60·771

f 183·425 + 84·04 + 8·777

g 71·823 + 614·4 + 8·003

h 823·14 + 85·744 + 5831·5

i 63·75 + 444·8 + 1005·7

j 76·14 + 7·88 + 8·152

k 9002·4 + 71·312 + 8·459

l 6·77 + 5·162 + 7824·3

m 1963·4 + 853·72 + 74·63

n 8·774 + 64·9 + 1532·23

o 20·44 + 81·753 + 6073·2

p 13·651 + 4·09 + 102·45

2 Choose four calculations and check your answers on a calculator.

3 Choose two calculations and make up a word problem involving measures.

Using the digits 4, 5, 6, 7, 8 and 9 make these totals by adding two numbers together. In each calculation each digit may only be used once.

a 10·596

b 66·36

c 485·4

d 73·29

e 13·26

f 104·34

Example

To make 77·25
I need to add

  7·85

 69·4

 77·25

  1 1

11

More vertical decimals

● **Use efficient written methods to subtract decimals**

 1 Write the number that goes with each decimal to equal 10.

a 5·1	d 9·5	g 3·3	j 6·5
b 8·6	e 1·8	h 7·9	k 0·6
c 7·4	f 2·7	i 1·4	l 5·4

2 Write out each calculation vertically and work out the answer.

Example

$$\begin{array}{r} {}^{1}\cancel{1}4\,{}^{6}8\cdot{}^{1}7\,3 \\ -\ 65\cdot47 \\ \hline 83\cdot26 \end{array}$$

Remember

● Include the decimal point in the answer!

● Make an estimate of your answer first.

a 84·67 – 52·36	i 28·624 – 15·814
b 157·8 – 106·2	j 751·44 – 108·19
c 97·481 – 26·381	k 67·48 – 20·67
d 204·8 – 38·9	l 821·7 – 59·3
e 187·61 – 57·16	m 196·72 – 80·39
f 319·57 – 126·38	n 75·19 – 26·24
g 167·82 – 67·08	o 181·75 – 84·66
h 483·91 – 76·37	

1 Write out each calculation vertically and work out the answer.

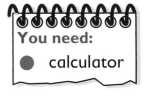
You need:
● calculator

a 7542·8 – 634·87

b 479·21 – 51·8

c 6372·8 – 483·69

d 4805·1 – 698·83

e 843·9 – 25·167

f 739·14 – 73·662

g 7114·5 – 43·81

h 507·43 – 77·327

i 1068·6 – 106·49

j 29 736·74 – 452·8

k 891·542 – 38·4

l 7810·6 – 521·66

m 652·94 – 48·61

n 6732·4 – 298·72

2 Choose four calculations and check your answers on a calculator.

3 Choose two calculations and write a word problem involving money.

Work out what needs to be subtracted from each number
to get to the next number. Record your answers as calculations.

a 426·75 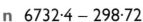 207·17 ➡ 159·72 ➡ 28·42

b 84·279 ➡ 51·437 ➡ 23·718 ➡ 9·104

c 1573·5 ➡ 954·8 ➡ 504·7 ➡ 331·6

Villa division

Write a division fact for each number coming out of the machine and give the answer.

a
| 81 |
| 45 |
| 63 |
| 27 |
| 72 |

÷9

b
| 36 |
| 24 |
| 16 |
| 40 |
| 32 |

÷4

c
| 14 |
| 63 |
| 49 |
| 21 |
| 56 |

÷7

d
| 30 |
| 42 |
| 18 |
| 36 |
| 54 |

÷6

e
| 24 |
| 21 |
| 9 |
| 15 |
| 27 |

÷3

f
| 16 |
| 32 |
| 72 |
| 24 |
| 48 |

÷8

Italy – Villa costs (per apartment, per week)			
	2 or 3 people	4, 5 or 6 people	7, 8 or 9 people
18 Mar – 14 Apr	295	385	445
15 Apr – 28 Apr	320	410	470
29 Apr – 23 Jun	355	430	485
24 Jun – 21 July	375	455	515
22 July – 18 Aug	630	750	865
19 Aug – 01 Sept	450	515	630
02 Sept – 29 Sept	390	450	505
30 Sep – 27 Oct	305	395	450

The travel agency has villas in Italy for rent. The cost of the villa depends on how many people will be staying and the date on which they travel. The agency has had many enquiries.

Work out how much it will cost each person in the group.

Record your answer using the short division method.

Enquiry No: 1
Date of travel: 20 April
No of people: 6
Length of stay: 1 week
Villa cost:
Cost per person:

Enquiry No: 2
Date of travel: 27 July
No of people: 9
Length of stay: 1 week
Villa cost:
Cost per person:

Enquiry No: 3
Date of travel: 12 August
No of people: 6
Length of stay: 1 week
Villa cost:
Cost per person:

Enquiry No: 4
Date of travel: 20 May
No of people: 3
Length of stay: 1 week
Villa cost:
Cost per person:

Enquiry No: 5
Date of travel: 31 August
No of people: 6
Length of stay: 1 week
Villa cost:
Cost per person:

Enquiry No: 6
Date of travel: 12 October
No of people: 5
Length of stay: 1 week
Villa cost:
Cost per person:

Enquiry No: 7
Date of travel: 15 August
No of people: 8
Length of stay: 2 weeks
Villa cost:
Cost per person:

Enquiry No: 8
Date of travel: 3 July
No of people: 7
Length of stay: 3 weeks
Villa cost:
Cost per person:

Enquiry No: 9
Date of travel: 27 June
No of people: 5
Length of stay: 4 weeks
Villa cost:
Cost per person:

What to do

Work with a partner

1 Take turns to roll the four dice. Choose one die as the divisor and put it to one side.

2 Using the remaining 3 dice, both players make the largest 3-digit number possible.

3 Divide the 3-digit number by the divisor. Show your working and write any remainders as a mixed number.

4 Check your answer with your partner's work.

You need:

● four 0–9 dice

Example

divisor 6) 743
600 (6 × 100)
143
120 (6 × 20)
23
18 (6 × 3)
5

Answer = $123\frac{5}{6}$

Lottie's allotment

 Approximate the answer to each calculation.

a	34·3 ÷ 3	g	39·6 ÷ 4	m	79·6 ÷ 9
b	64·7 ÷ 6	h	57·4 ÷ 8	n	56·3 ÷ 10
c	46·8 ÷ 5	i	32·5 ÷ 5	o	28·7 ÷ 2
d	28·3 ÷ 4	j	28·7 ÷ 3	p	46·2 ÷ 7
e	37·5 ÷ 7	k	83·6 ÷ 9	q	39·7 ÷ 8
f	16·8 ÷ 9	l	47·2 ÷ 8	r	66·2 ÷ 9

1 Lottie marks out a row in the soil 1 m long.

She places lettuce seedlings 20 cm apart along the row.

How many lettuces does she plant in one row?

2 She has 6 potatoes to plant in a row 1·5 m long.

Find the length of gap in centimetres between each potato.

3 Lottie has 13 cabbage seedlings.
The row is 0·96 m long.

Find how far apart each plant is.

4 Lottie has marked out a row 225 cm long for her sweet pea plants.

She leaves a gap of 9 cm between each plant.

How many sweet pea plants does she have?

5 Lottie kept a record of how her plants had grown over several weeks.

Work out how much each plant grew, on average, in one week.

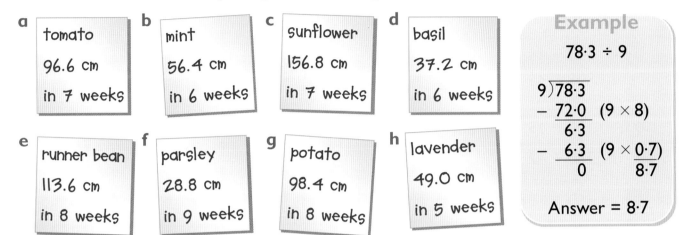

a tomato 96.6 cm in 7 weeks

b mint 56.4 cm in 6 weeks

c sunflower 156.8 cm in 7 weeks

d basil 37.2 cm in 6 weeks

Example

78·3 ÷ 9

```
   _____
9)78·3
 − 72·0  (9 × 8)
   ────
    6·3
 −  6·3  (9 × 0·7)
    ───
      0      8·7
```

Answer = 8·7

e runner bean 113.6 cm in 8 weeks

f parsley 28.8 cm in 9 weeks

g potato 98.4 cm in 8 weeks

h lavender 49.0 cm in 5 weeks

Rearrange each set of 4 numbers to make a calculation in the form $\boxed{\text{TU·t ÷ U}}$ to equal the answer shown on each label.

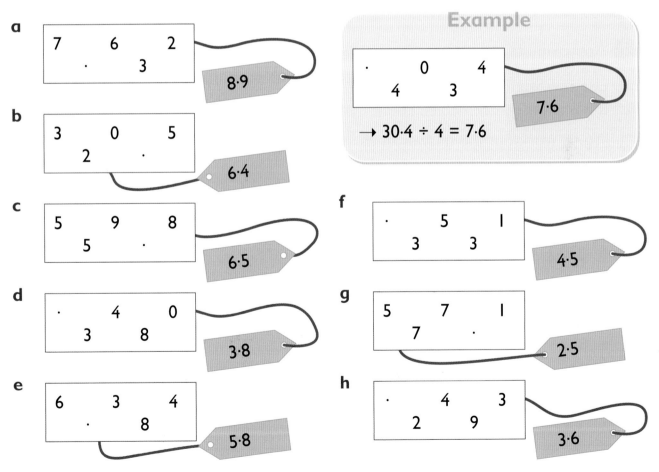

Example

| . | 0 | 4 |
| 4 | | 3 |

→ 30.4 ÷ 4 = 7.6

7·6

a

| 7 | 6 | 2 |
| . | 3 | |

8·9

b

| 3 | 0 | 5 |
| 2 | . | |

6·4

c

| 5 | 9 | 8 |
| 5 | . | |

6·5

d

| . | 4 | 0 |
| 3 | 8 | |

3·8

e

| 6 | 3 | 4 |
| . | 8 | |

5·8

f

| . | 5 | 1 |
| 3 | 3 | |

4·5

g

| 5 | 7 | 1 |
| 7 | . | |

2·5

h

| . | 4 | 3 |
| 2 | 9 | |

3·6

17

Long division

● **Use effiecient written methods to divide whole numbers**

Work out the answers to these in your head.

1 a 150 ÷ 15   c 320 ÷ 32   e 240 ÷ 24

    b 270 ÷ 27   d 120 ÷ 12   f 350 ÷ 35

2 a 300 ÷ 15   c 360 ÷ 18   e 280 ÷ 14

    b 240 ÷ 12   d 400 ÷ 20   f 460 ÷ 23

3 a 450 ÷ 15   c 480 ÷ 12   e 440 ÷ 11

    b 750 ÷ 25   d 390 ÷ 13   f 690 ÷ 23

4 a 770 ÷ 11   c 600 ÷ 12   e 450 ÷ 50

    b 640 ÷ 32   d 540 ÷ 60   f 280 ÷ 40

 1 Approximate the answer first.

Use a written method to work out the answer to each calculation.

Try to work out the answer in as few steps as possible using multiples of 10 multiplied by the divisor.

a 754 ÷ 13   h 992 ÷ 32

b 930 ÷ 15   i 952 ÷ 34

c 912 ÷ 24   j 989 ÷ 43

d 884 ÷ 26   k 864 ÷ 54

e 882 ÷ 18   l 900 ÷ 25

f 969 ÷ 17   m 768 ÷ 48

g 957 ÷ 29   n 924 ÷ 33

A school's electricity bill for half the year is £832.

What is the cost per week?

We can write this as a calculation:

832 ÷ 26 = ☐

We can work it out like this:

832 ÷ 26 ≈ 900 ÷ 30 = 30

$$
\begin{array}{r}
26\overline{)832} \\
- 780 \quad 26 \times 30 \\
\hline
52 \\
- 52 \quad 26 \times 2 \\
\hline
0 \qquad\qquad 32 \\
\end{array}
$$

Answer = 32

The total cost per week is £32.

18

2 Find the answers to these word problems using the method on page 18.

a A carton contains 672 pencils.

Each box holds 12 pencils.

How many boxes are there in the carton?

b The total bill for 24 nights hotel accommodation is £936.

How much does it cost per night?

c The Football Club has a lottery syndicate made up of 23 people.

One week they win £966.

How much does each person receive?

d A car uses 882 l of petrol a fortnight.

How many litres does it use on average per day?

Calculate the answers to these.

Reduce any remainder to its simplest form.

Example

$$595 \div 21 = 28 \text{ r } 7 = 28 \frac{7}{21} = 28 \frac{1}{3}$$

a $870 \div 24$

b $825 \div 12$

c $1365 \div 25$

d $1032 \div 16$

e $1320 \div 36$

f $1662 \div 42$

g $879 \div 18$

h $1720 \div 48$

i $2110 \div 40$

More long division

Write the first 5 multiples of each of these numbers.

a
16

e
22

i
70

m
24

Example

12 →12, 24, 36, 48, 60

b
25

f
31

j
15

n
50

c
14

g
40

k
90

o
13

q
80

s
61

d
9

h
52

l
33

p
42

r
35

t
65

  1 Approximate the answer first.

Choose a written method to work out the answer to each calculation.

Remember

Remember to keep the numbers in the correct columns.

Example

$555 \div 15 \approx 600 \div 15 = 40$

```
    ┌─────
15 )555
  −  450    15 × 30
    ─────
     105
  −  105    15 × 7
    ─────
       0
```

Answer = 37

or

Example

$555 \div 15 \approx 600 \div 15 = 40$

```
       37
    ┌─────
15 )555
  −  450
    ─────
     105
  −  105
    ─────
       0
```

Answer = 37

a

768 ÷ 16

b

621 ÷ 23

c

992 ÷ 32

d

931 ÷ 19

e
850 ÷ 25

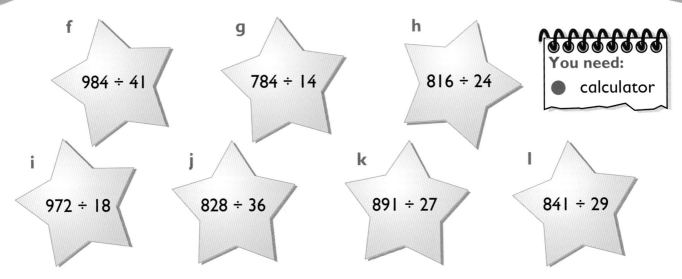

f 984 ÷ 41

g 784 ÷ 14

h 816 ÷ 24

You need:
● calculator

i 972 ÷ 18

j 828 ÷ 36

k 891 ÷ 27

l 841 ÷ 29

2 Use a multiplication calculation to check your answers.

Record what calculation you used to check each answer.

Example

555 ÷ 15 = [37] 🖩 → 37 × 15 = 555

1 49 is the answer to 5 of these calculations.

Can you find them?

1127 ÷ 23

882 ÷ 18

588 ÷ 12

1296 ÷ 27

1104 ÷ 24

1225 ÷ 25

1764 ÷ 36

2 Which of these numbers are divisible by 16?

304

388

944

824

1344

720

1008

1258

Working in Lottie's allotment

Solve multi-step problems

1 List the multiples of 6 between 30 and 100.

2 Take each number from the box and divide it by 6.

Find the remainder R and write the number on the correct remainder line.

R1 ....

R2 ....

R3 ....

R4 ....

R5 ....

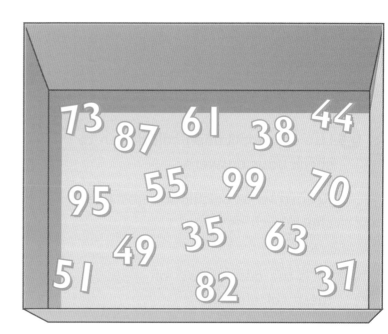

73 87 61 38 44

95 55 99 70

49 35 63

51 82 37

1 Lottie has produce to sell at the farmers' market.

Estimate then calculate how many trays and bags she needs for each item.

a
```
tomatoes
6 per tray
number picked: 144
```

b
```
mushrooms
8 per tray
number picked: 136
```

c
```
runner beans
25 per tray
number picked: 475
```

d
```
carrots
9 per bag
number picked: 234
```

e
```
onions
12 per bag
number picked: 216
```

f
```
plums
15 per bag
number picked: 495
```

2 Work out mentally how many of each vegetable Lottie sold at the market.

a
lettuce

29p each

total sales £11.60

b
cucumber

35p each

total sales £10.50

c
parsley

15p per bunch

total sales £4.50

3 Lottie is building a new fence at the back of her allotment.

She has a supply of posts and trellis boards.

They are fixed together like this:

2 posts,
2 trellis boards

3 posts,
4 trellis boards

a How many trellis boards does she need for 10 posts?

b Find a rule.

c Write it as a formula that connects the posts (P) and the trellis boards (T).

d She orders 30 trellis boards from the DIY store. How many posts does she order?

The leaves on Lottie's runner beans are arranged helically around the stem so that they do not screen each other from the sunlight.

Fibonacci, an Italian mathematician, found this sequence of numbers for the leaves of certain plants.

1, 1, 2, 3, 5, 8, 13, 21, ... , ... , ...

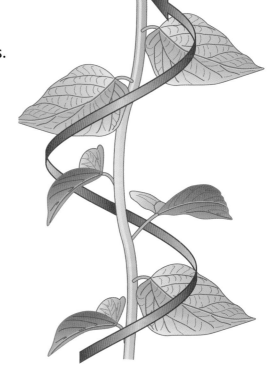

1 Complete the next 3 numbers in the sequence.

2 Take 4 'next door' Fibonacci numbers: 2, 3, 5, 8

● Multiply the two outside numbers.

● Multiply the two inside numbers.

● Find the difference.

3 Investigate for 5, 8, 13, 21 and then for 13, 21, ... , ...

Write what you notice.

Multiplying mentally

● Use multiplication facts to work out mentally other facts involving decimals

Find the answers to these calculations. Show your working.

a 22 × 14

b 43 × 12

c 35 × 11

d 24 × 16

e 26 × 16

f 44 × 13

g 32 × 18

h 19 × 17

i 23 × 16

j 25 × 19

Example

24 × 14 = (24 × 10) + (24 × 4)

= 240 + 96

= 336

1 Copy and complete.

a 84 × 100 = 8400

  84 × 101 = 8484

  8·4 × 101 =

  0·84 × 101 =

b 57 × 100 =

  57 × 101 =

  5·7 × 101 =

  0·57 × 101 =

c 96 × 100 =

  96 × 101 =

  9·6 × 101 =

  0·96 × 101 =

2 Find the answers to these calculations. Show your working.

a 3·2 × 16

b 8·5 × 14

c 1·9 × 12

d 2·7 × 15

e 6·4 × 18

f 9·8 × 30

g 2·8 × 25

h 4·1 × 24

i 7·3 × 21

j 5·6 × 80

Example

Partitioning

2·4 × 14 = (2·4 × 10) + (2·4 × 4)

= 24 + 9·6

= 33·6

Using factors

2·4 × 14 = (2·4 × 7) × 2

= 16·8 × 2

= 33·6

24

3 **a** Copy and complete.

$1·85 \times 2 \times 3 =$

$1·85 \times 4 \times 3 =$

$1·85 \times 6 \times 3 =$

$1·85 \times 8 \times 3 =$

b Use the pattern to work out these:

$1.85 \times 12 \times 3 =$

$1·85 \times 14 \times 3 =$

$1·85 \times 16 \times 3 =$

$1·85 \times 18 \times 3 =$

c Use your answers in **b** to work out these:

$18·5 \times 12 \times 3 =$

$185 \times 14 \times 3 =$

$0·185 \times 16 \times 3 =$

$0·0185 \times 18 \times 3 =$

| 2 | 3 | 4 | 5 | 6 |

Take four of the above five numbers.

Using each number once, fit them into this calculation.

$$(\boxed{} - \boxed{}) \times (\boxed{} + \boxed{}) = 16$$

Find all the possible solutions.

Dividing mentally

● Use division facts to work out mentally other facts involving decimals

Copy the table and follow these steps.

Step 1: Write the calculation and answer in column 1.

Step 2: Check with an inverse operation in column 2.

Step 3: Derive the answer for column 3 from column 1.

Example

$36 \div 4 = 9$

$9 \times 4 = 36$

$3 \cdot 6 \div 4 = 0 \cdot 9$

1 Calculate	2 Check			3 Derive
$56 \div 4 =$	....	×	=	$5 \cdot 6 \div 4 =$
$91 \div 7 =$	....	×	=	$9 \cdot 1 \div 7 =$
$96 \div 6 =$	....	×	=	$9 \cdot 6 \div 6 =$
$85 \div 5 =$	....	×	=	$8 \cdot 5 \div 5 =$
$102 \div 3 =$	....	×	=	$10 \cdot 2 \div 3 =$
$144 \div 9 =$	....	×	=	$14 \cdot 4 \div 9 =$
$175 \div 5 =$	....	×	=	$17 \cdot 5 \div 5 =$
$156 \div 6 =$	....	×	=	$15 \cdot 6 \div 6 =$

 1 Using factors, find the answers to the calculations.

Show your working.

a $224 \div 14 =$

b $288 \div 16 =$

c $432 \div 12 =$

d $396 \div 18 =$

e $600 \div 25 =$

f $870 \div 15 =$

g $608 \div 16 =$

h $903 \div 21 =$

i $648 \div 27 =$

j $735 \div 35 =$

Example

$336 \div 16 = (336 \div 2) \div 8$

$= 168 \div 8$

$= 21$

Check by reversing factors

$336 \div 16 = (336 \div 8) \div 2$

$= 42 \div 2$

$= 21$

Check each answer by reversing the pair of factors.

2 Using factors, find the answers to the calculations.

Show your working.

408 km ÷ 12 =   675 kg ÷ 25 =   5321 ÷ 14 =

40·8 km ÷ 12 =   67·5 kg ÷ 25 =   53·21 ÷ 14 =

4·08 km ÷ 12 =   6·75 kg ÷ 25 =   5·321 ÷ 14 =

3 Halving game

A game for 2 players

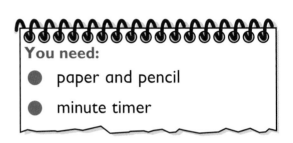

You need:
- paper and pencil
- minute timer

What to do

- Take turns to choose one of the numbers.
- Both players write the number down.
- Start the timer.
- Halve the number and keep halving until the minute is up.
- Compare answers.
- The person with the most correct answers scores 1 point.
- The first person to score 5 points is the winner.

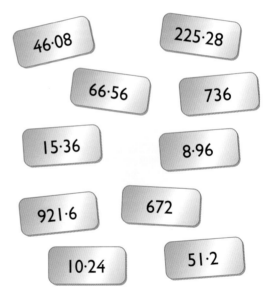

46·08   225·28

66·56   736

15·36   8·96

921·6   672

10·24   51·2

1 Use your calculator to work out the answer to these calculations.

(77·31 − 71·06) × (6·86 + 9·14)   (86·2 + 77·5) − (34·8 + 28·9)

(38·11 + 99·39) ÷ (5·5 × 0·25)

You need:
- calculator

2 Write what you notice.

3 Make up a calculation with two sets of brackets which has a similar result.

Ask a friend to check it.

Using multiplication facts

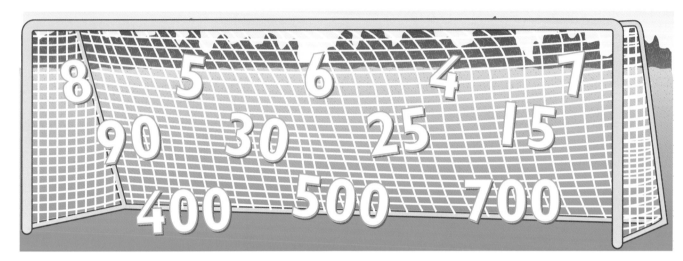

Multiply any two numbers from between the goal posts to give the number on each football.

a 450 b 200 c 105 d 3500 e 5600 f 4200

g 12 000 h 7500 i 63 000 j 2000 k 10 000 l 280 000

1 a Use an efficient written method to find the answer to 123 × 45.

b Use the digits 1, 2, 3, 4 and 5 once to make a 3-digit by a 2-digit multiplication that has the answer:

　i greater than 123 × 45

　ii smaller than 123 × 45

2 Draw a 2 x 2 grid.

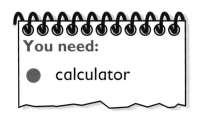

You need:
● calculator

Put the numbers 10, 15, 20 and 25 in the grid.

Multiply the adjacent numbers.

Total the products.

a Find the largest total.

b Find the smallest total.

c Use the grid arrangement to find the greatest total for:

  i 3^2, 4^2, 5^2 and 6^2.

  ii 10^2, 20^2, 30^2 and 40^2.

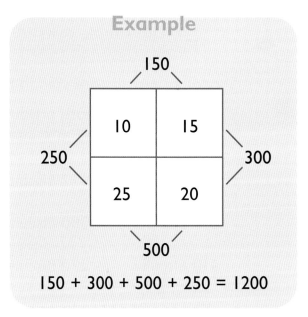

Example

$$150 + 300 + 500 + 250 = 1200$$

3 Put the digits 4, 5, 6 and 7 in the blank squares to complete each calculation.

Estimate first, then check with your calculator.

a ☐☐☐ × ☐ = 3822   **c** ☐☐☐ × ☐ = 2742

b ☐☐☐ × ☐ = 2700   **d** ☐☐☐ × ☐ = 3730

Work with a partner.

1 You have 4 digit cards:

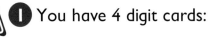

3 **5** **7** **8**

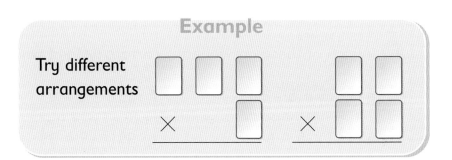

Example

Try different arrangements

Find the largest product you can make using all 4 cards.

2 Now find the smallest product you can make with the same 4 digits.

Look at your answers in question **1** to help you.

Divisibility

● **Use simple tests of divisibility**

Chocolate biscuits are sold in packets of 6.

a Decide which factory production runs can be put into packets of 6 exactly.

78 biscuits	112 biscuits	150 biscuits
135 biscuits	200 biscuits	184 biscuits
318 biscuits	270 biscuits	236 biscuits

> **Example**
>
> 144 biscuits
>
> 144 is even
>
> 1 + 4 + 4 = 9 = multiple of 3
>
> 144 divides by 6

b Which factory production runs can be put into packets of 9?

1 Copy and complete the table.

	÷ 2	÷ 3	÷ 4	÷ 5	÷ 6	÷ 8	÷ 9	÷ 10	÷ 25
123		✓							
720									
531									
2056			✓						
5454									
9675									

> **Example**
>
> 1 + 2 + 3 = 6
>
> 123 ÷ 3 ✓

> ✓ correct
> ✗ incorrect

2 Which of these answers are correct (✓) and which are incorrect (✗).

a 2725 ÷ 5 = 545

b 762 ÷ 9 = 84

c 536 ÷ 4 = 134

d 458 ÷ 3 = 151

e 664 ÷ 4 = 166

f 351 ÷ 4 = 89

g 891 ÷ 9 = 99

h 3650 ÷ 5 = 730

i 452 ÷ 3 = 164

j 2644 ÷ 2 = 1322

> **Example**
>
> 2725 ÷ 5 = 545 ✓

k 1125 ÷ 25 = 45

l 786 ÷ 9 = 78

3 Use this test of divisibility by 7 for 3-digit numbers.

- ● Double the hundreds digit.
- ● Add this to the two-digit number made from the tens and units digits.
- ● Is the total a multiple of 7?
- ● If yes, then the number is divisible by 7.

Example

371

$2 \times 3 = 6$

$6 + 71 = 77$

$77 \div 7 = 11$

371 divides by 7

a Check which of these numbers are divisible by 7.

343　　　　259　　　　　　406

686　　　　537　　　　　　580

b Find four 3-digit numbers greater than 800 that are divisible by 7.

White and dark chocolates come off the production line in a continuous pattern like this:

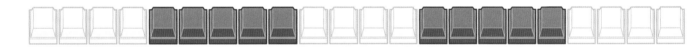

1 Find the colour of:

a the 68th chocolate

b the 47th chocolate

c the 110th chocolate

d the 214th chocolate

e the 500th chocolate

f the 678th chocolate

2 I am divisible by 7.

I am a 3-digit number.

My units digit is 3 times my hundreds digit.

All 3 digits are different.

What number am I?

Calculator puzzles

* Use a calculator to solve problems with more than one step

1 a Enter this key sequence into your calculator.

Record the three answers produced by the equals sign.

Repeat the above for these key sequences :

b

c

d    **f**

e    **g**

You need:
* calculator

Example

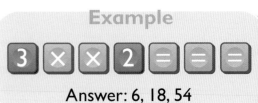

Answer: 6, 18, 54

2 Write about any patterns you notice.

 1 Copy and complete the table.

Calculator display	Money £	Length m and cm	Capacity l and ml	Time hrs and min
1·4	£1.40	1 m 40 cm	1 l 400 ml	1 hr 24 min
27·5				
38·75				
14·2				
9·6				

You need:
* calculator

2 For each calculation, estimate the answer as:

i More than 400 or   **ii** Less than 400

Then use your calculator to find the actual answer.

a 7·3 × 8·2 × 6·5   **b** (32·1 × 11) + (11 × 11)

c (24 × 20) − (2·4 × 15)   **d** 900 ÷ (11·9 − 9·5)

3 Follow these steps.

Display a 3-digit number on your calculator.

Repeat the same 3 digits to make a 6-digit number.

Divide by 7.

Divide by 11.

Divide by 13.

a Enter 10 different 3-digit numbers and record your findings.

b Write what you notice.

c Find a way to explain why this happens.

Example

257

257257

$\div 7 = 36751$

$\div 11 = 3341$

$\div 13 = 257$

HINT

Think about the inverse operation.

What did I do?

A game for 2 players

Rules

Shuffle the cards and place them face down in a pile.

The first player takes the top 3 cards and puts them face up on the table.

Without showing the other player, the first player makes a calculation on the calculator involving multiplication or division using the 3 digits.

Press [=] and show the answer to the second player.

Start the stopwatch or timer.

The second player has 1 minute to find the calculation.

Scoring

2 points to second player for working out the calculation.

1 point to first player if calculation cannot be worked out in time.

Winner is the first player to score 10 points.

You need:

- a set of 0-9 digit cards
- calculator
- stopwatch or minute timer

Example

3   7   6

$3 \times 7 \times 6 = 126$

$7 \times 6 \div 3 = 14$

$37 \times 6 = 222$

$76 \div 3 = 25.3333$

$7.3 \times 6 = 43.8$

$0.7 \times 0.3 \times 6 = 1.26$

Find the missing numbers

 Use the numbers 1–10 to make these statements correct.

For each number sentence a different letter indicates a different number.

 1 2 3 4 5 6 7 8 9 10

1. $A \times A = 16$

2. $B + B + B = 15$

3. $4 \times C = 24$

4. $D \times D = 30 + D$

5. $E + 25 = 34$

6. $F \times 15 = 30$

7. $G \times G \times G = 8$

8. $H + H + H = 9$

9. $J \times J \times J = J$

10. $K \times K + K = 110$

11. $40 - L - L - L - L = 0$

12. $M + M + M = N + N$

13. $P \times P = 72 - P$

14. $T \times T + T = 42$

 Here are some multiplication tables for you to try.

They are in code and each letter represents a different number. (Each table has a different set of values for its letters.)

1. Can you work out which multiplication table belongs to each of the following tables?

2. Write an explanation of how you worked out your answer for each one.

Table ▣

$A \times K = K$	$A \times F = F$	$A \times B = B$
$A \times S = S$	$A \times A = A$	$A \times G = G$
$A \times Y = Y$	$A \times L = L$	$A \times M = M$

Table ▲

Z × A = TL

Z × K = Z

Z × Z = DK

Z × B = NC

Z × N = KD

Z × C = AB

Z × D = CN

Z × L = BA

Z × T = LT

Table ●

S × A = FA

S × B = CD

S × C = G

S × D = CF

S × S = B

S × F = S

S × G = FJ

S × H = FC

S × J = CH

Table ◆

J × Z = UZ

J × Y = RQ

J × W = YT

J × V = TZ

J × U = J

J × J = RJ

J × S = TS

J × R = US

J × T = ZT

Valuable words

1 Write the letters A–Z in order.

2 Give each letter a number from 1 to 26 in order, so A = 1, B = 2, …

You need:

● calculator where appropriate

3 What is the sum of each of these words?

EXPENSIVE   THOUSAND   AUTUMN   CHRISTMAS

4 What is the product of each of these words?

TIMES   SUMMER   COMPUTE   MILLION

> **Example**
> ONE = 15 + 14 + 5 = 34

5 Can you find a word that has a value of 100?

> **Example**
> ONE = 15 × 14 × 5 = 1050

6 How many words can you find with a value of 1000? (You can mix operations and use brackets.)

Consecutive numbers

a Find the numbers you can make, up to 40, by adding pairs of consecutive numbers. Record your results in an organised list.

b Copy and complete this statement.

You can make .... numbers except .... by adding 2 consecutive numbers.

c Write which numbers in your list are square numbers.

d Which of these numbers can you make by adding pairs of consecutive numbers?

36   49   64   81

Example

1 + 2 = 3

2 + 3 = 5

3 + 4

HINT

Use what you found in b.

 1 a Jordan said: 'You can make 43 numbers between 1 and 50 by adding consecutive numbers.'

True or false? Investigate.

Example

4 + 5 = 9

7 + 8 + 9 = 24

You need:

● calculator

b List the numbers Jordan could not make and find a link between them.

2 Find 4 consecutive numbers which total:

a 34   **c** 78   **e** 206

b 54   **d** 142   **f** 186

Show all your working.

You can use a calculator to help you.

Example

2 + 3 + 4 + 5 = 14

2 + 3 + 4 + 5 + 6 + 7 = 27

3 Jennifer wrote a rule for consecutive numbers:

> **Rule:**
>
> Take any 3 consecutive numbers, square the middle number, and the product is always 1 more than the product of the other 2 numbers.

a Use your calculator to test Jennifer's rule 6 times.

Choose a range of 3 consecutive numbers.

Record your calculations.

b Write what you notice.

c Will the rule work for these numbers? Check.

124, 125, 126   249, 250, 251   332, 333, 334

1, 3, 5, 7 and 9 are five consecutive alternate numbers.
Their total is 25.

2, 4, 6, 8 and 10 are five consecutive alternate numbers.
Their total is 30.

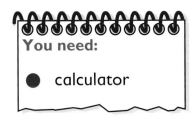

You need:
● calculator

1 a Find the five consecutive alternate numbers which have these totals.

i 50   ii 85   iii 110

iv 175   v 200   vi 345

b Find a quick way of working out the five numbers without having to add them.
Write it as a rule.

2 Now find seven consecutive numbers which total:

a 28   b 56   c 105   d 308

Prime number puzzles

Find which numbers less than 100 are prime

You need:

● squared paper

1 a Copy the grid on to squared paper.

   b Circle all the prime numbers on your grid.

2 In which columns do the prime numbers after 5 appear?

3 Using this pattern, list the next 5 prime numbers.

4 Find 2 prime numbers which total these even numbers.

1	2	3	4	5	6
7	8	9	10	11	12
13	14	15	16	17	18
19	20	21	22	23	24
25	26	27	28	29	30
31	32	33	34	35	36
37	38	39	40	41	42
43	44	45	46	47	48
49	50	51	52	53	54
55	56	57	58	59	60
61	62	63	64	65	66
67	68	69	70	71	72

a   b   c

12   32   36

d   e   f

52   68   72

Example

8   8 = 5 + 3

5 3

5 Find 2 pairs of prime numbers, each of which will total these even numbers.

   a   16 = 3 + ...   b   28 =   c   46 =

          = 5 + ...

1 a Copy the grid on to squared paper and extend to 102.

You need:
- squared paper
- calculator

1	2	3	4	5	6
7	8	9	10	11	12
13	14	15	16	17	18
19	20	21	22	23	24
25	26	27	28	29	
31	32	33			

b Circle all the prime numbers.

c Put a cross on every number that is 1 more or 1 less than a multiple of 6.

Write what you notice.

2 16 is a square number that is the sum of 2 prime numbers.

Find all the pairs of prime numbers that total:

a 6^2 **b** 8^2

Example

$16 = 13 + 3$

or $= 11 + 5$

3 Find all the ways of making 6 by subtracting two consecutive prime numbers less than 100.

4 Choose 10 prime numbers between 6 and 100.

For each number:
- Square the prime number;
- Divide by 12;
- Write the remainder.

Write what you notice.

Example

$47^2 = 2209$

$2209 \div 12 = 184 \text{ R } 1$

Remainder $= 1$

0 1 2 3 4 5 6 7 8 9

Use all 10 cards to make 5 prime numbers.

At least one prime number must be a 3-digit number.

Try to find three possible answers.

Use a calculator to check.

You need:
- 0-9 digit cards
- calculator

Example

2   8 9

5   3 0 7

4 6 1

Goldbach's conjecture

The children in Year 6 carried out an  *investigation*

All prime numbers occur as pairs of odd numbers

Can you find any other pairs of consecutive odd numbers up to 100 that are prime numbers?

Here are some of their results.

5, 7
11, 13
17, 19
29, 31

Conjecture

1 An opinion formed based on incomplete information.

2 An opinion or conclusion reached through incomplete information.

Christian Goldbach (1690–1764) was a Professor of Mathematics at the Russian Imperial Academy.

He made the conjecture that:

> Every even number greater than 2 is the sum of two prime numbers.

1 List the even numbers from 4 to 50.

2 Can each of these numbers be expressed as the sum of two prime numbers?

3 Do some of the even numbers have more than one solution?

4 Which number has the greatest collection of pairs of prime numbers that make its total?

5 Can you find any even number that is not the sum of 2 prime numbers?

4 = 2 + 2
6 = 3 + 3
8 = 3 + 5
10 = 3 + 7, 5 + 5
12 = ...
14 = . . . , ...

Try out random even numbers up to 100. Does Goldbach's conjecture work? What about random numbers up to 200?

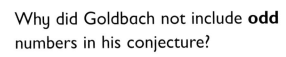

Why did Goldbach not include **odd** numbers in his conjecture?

Is every odd number the sum of two prime numbers?

1 Make a list of odd numbers from 5 up to 49.

2 Can every odd number be expressed as the sum of 2 prime numbers?

3 What do you notice?

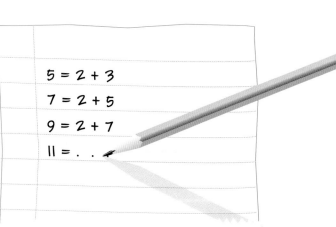

5 = 2 + 3
7 = 2 + 5
9 = 2 + 7
11 = . . .

Extending the pattern

  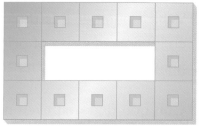

a Make the next three patterns in the sequence with centicubes.

b Copy and complete the table.

Pattern number (P)	1	2	3	4	5	6
Number of cubes (N)	8					

You need:
● centicubes

c Look for a pattern. Use it to find the number of centicubes in the 10th pattern.

1 Copy the dot sequence and draw the next two patterns in the sequence.

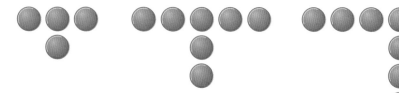

2 a Copy and complete the table.

Pattern number (P)	1	2	3	4	5	100
Number of dots (D)						

You need:
● counters (optional)

b Find a rule and write it as a formula.

c Use the formula to find how many dots will be in the 100th pattern of the sequence. Record your answer in the table.

3 Find the number of dots in the 100th pattern of these sequences.

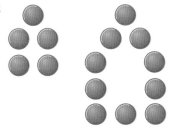

a

b

c

d

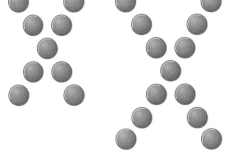

1 a Find the sum of the numbers in the 100th row of this array.

1

3 + 5

7 + 9 + 11

13 + 15 + 17 + 19

21 + 23 + 25 + 27 + 29

b Copy and complete the table.

Row number (R)	1	2	3	4	5	100
Sum (S)						

2 a Find the sum of the numbers in the 100th row of this array. Look to the pattern in the first table for help.

2

4 + 6

8 + 10 + 12

14 + 16 + 18 + 20

22 + 24 + 26 + 28 + 30

b Copy and complete the table.

Row number (R)	1	2	3	4	5	100
Sum (S)						

3-D edges and faces

This is a wall cupboard in the kitchen.

The corners of the door are labelled A, B, C and D.

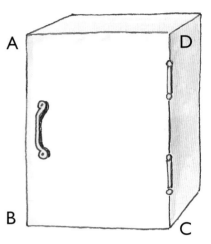

① Copy and complete these sentences.

   a The horizontal edges are AD and ....

   b The vertical edges are .... and ....

   c Edge AD is parallel to ....

   d Edge .... is parallel to AB.

② Name 2 pairs of perpendicular edges.

The table is horizontal.

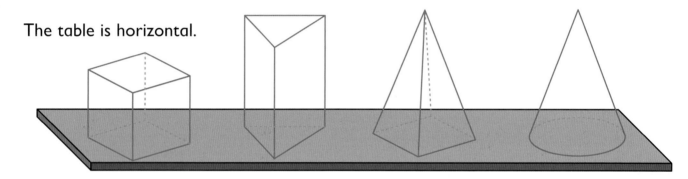

| cube | triangular prism | square-based pyramid | cone |

① a For each solid, write the total number of faces.

   b Count the number of faces which are horizontal and which are vertical.

Remember

In some solids there will be faces which are neither horizontal nor vertical.

Copy and complete this table

Solid	Total number of faces	Horizontal faces	Vertical faces
cube	6	2	
triangular prism			
square-based pyramid			
cone			

2 Copy and complete this table for the edges of each solid.

Solid	Total number of edges	Horizontal edges	Vertical edges
cube	12		
triangular prism			
square-based pyramid			
cone			

3 These solids are on a horizontal shelf.

For each shape:

a name 2 pairs of parallel edges.

b name 4 pairs of perpendicular edges.

c write the number of faces which are perpendicular to the shelf.

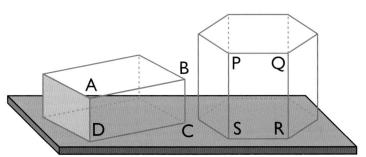

These solids are on a horizontal table.

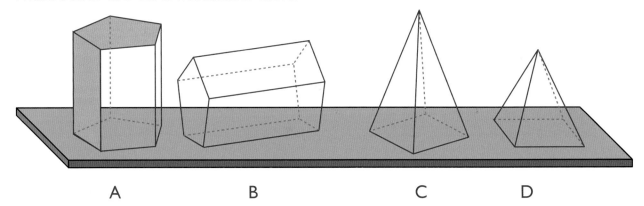

Work with a partner.

1 a Make a table to list the number of **horizontal** and **perpendicular** faces for each pentagonal prism (shapes A and B) and each pyramid (shapes C and D).

b Compare your answers for the pentagonal prisms, then for the pyramids.
Write what you notice.

2 a Make a table to list the number of pairs of parallel edges for each solid.

b Write what you notice about your answers for solids A and B, then solids C and D.

Nets of 3-D solids

| cube | regular tetrahedron | square-based pyramid | pentagonal pyramid |

   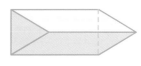

| octahedron | dodecahedron | cuboid | triangular prism |

Work with a partner. For each question, write into which region, 1, 2 or 3, you would sort these solids:

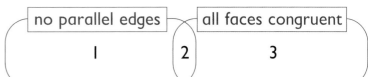

| no parallel edges | all faces congruent |
| 1 | 2 | 3 |

a cube, regular tetrahedron, octahedron, pentagonal pyramid

b dodecahedron, triangular prism, square-based pyramid, cuboid

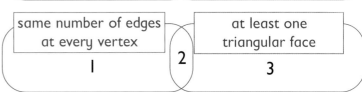

| same number of edges at every vertex | at least one triangular face |
| 1 | 2 | 3 |

1. Work in a group. Copy the net of a hexagonal prism on to 1 cm triangular dot paper. Make 7 hexagonal prisms altogether.

2. Cut out the net in one piece and cut along the thick lines sloping inwards.

3. For each net:
   ● score all dotted lines before folding
   ● stick face A over face B
   ● bend the flaps 1 to 6 and 7 to 12 inwards
   ● stick down faces C and D over the flaps.

You need:
● 1 cm triangular dot paper
● ruler
● scissors
● glue
● Blu-tack

4 Join the 7 prisms together with Blu-tack to make another hexagonal prism.

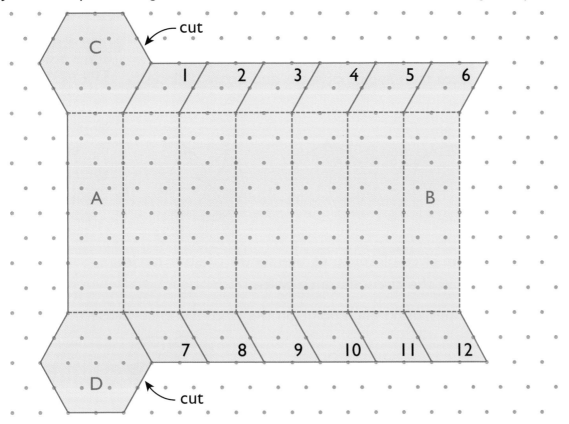

1 Work with a partner. Each person draws and cuts out the net of a square-based pyramid.

2 Find a way to glue the pieces together to make a 'snap dragon' octahedron. Add the teeth and the eyes.

You need:

- 1 cm triangular dot paper
- ruler
- scissors
- glue
- colouring materials

Circle patterns

● **Make shapes with increasing accuracy**

1 Construct a basic 'hex' pattern.

a Set your compasses to a radius of 4 cm and draw a circle.

b Mark off the radius around the circumference.

You need:
● compasses
● ruler
● eraser
● colouring
materials

c Use a mark on the circumference as the centre of your circle.
Draw an arc to cut the circumference twice.

d Repeat 5 more times, using each point on the circumference. Erase the unwanted lines.

2 These designs are based on the 'hex' pattern.

Choose one to construct and colour.

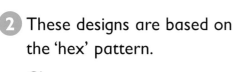

1 a Find the middle of your sheet of 1 cm square dot paper. Set your compasses to a radius of 5 cm and draw a circle. Mark the centre O.

You need:
● 1 cm square dot paper
● compasses
● ruler
● eraser
● colouring materials

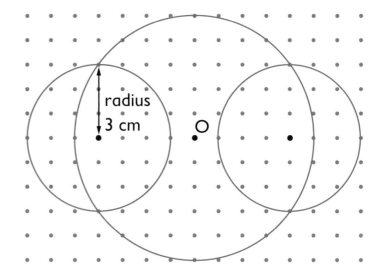

radius
3 cm

48

b Draw two circles, each with a centre 4 cm from O and with a radius of 3 cm.

c Draw two more circles, moving the centres 1 cm nearer to O and with a radius of 4 cm.

d Draw another pair of circles, moving the centres 1 cm nearer to O and with a radius of 5 cm.

e Colour part of your design.

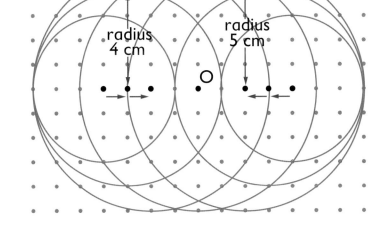

2 Design a similar pattern of your own.

1 Find a way to construct this basic pattern. PQRS is a square with sides of 6 cm. P, Q, R and S are the centres of circles with radius of 4·2 cm.

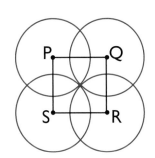

You need:
- compasses
- protractor or set square
- eraser
- ruler
- colouring materials

2 These designs are constructed from the basic pattern.

Work out how each design has been made. Choose two to construct and colour.

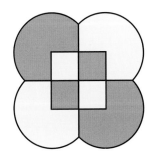

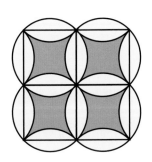

Rotating designs

1 a Find the centre of each square by drawing in the diagonals.

20 cm   10 cm

b Draw a circle with a radius of 5 cm.

Divide the circle into 30° sectors.

c Line up the vertex of the smaller square with a radius.

Draw around the square lightly in pencil.

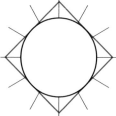

c Rotate the square until the vertex lines up with the next radius. Draw round the square.

Repeat once more for the small square.

2 Repeat **1** b–d for the larger square, drawing a circle of radius 10 cm. Colour your pattern.

1 Draw a circle with a radius of 5 cm and construct a basic 'hex' pattern.

Draw all lines lightly, because some will be erased later.

Follow these steps to make your design.

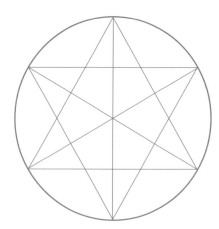

Erase the circle...

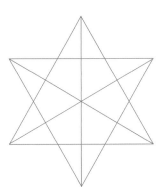

draw a hex pattern inside the first . . .

erase some lines.

Finish with this design . . .

or this one.

2 Colour your pattern to make a rotating shape.

3 Start with a basic 'hex' pattern and make your own rotating design.

 Using the basic 'hex' pattern, find a way to construct these designs.

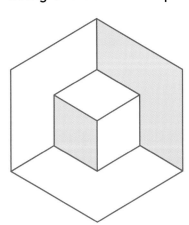

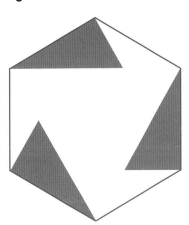

You need:
- compasses
- ruler
- colouring materials

Looking at 3-D solids

Make shapes with increasing accuracy

1 Work as a group to cut out 1 large and 4 small tetrahedron nets.

2 For each net:
- score all lines before folding.
- glue the tabs in turn.

3 Mark the mid point of each edge of the large tetrahedron.

4 For each face of the large tetrahedron, line up the vertices of the small tetrahedron with the marks and glue it in place.

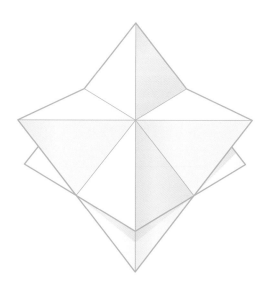

1 Work with a partner. Each person copies the net of a half-tetrahedron on to 1 cm triangular dot paper.

2 Carefully cut out the net.

3 For each net:
- score all dotted lines before folding.
- fold up before gluing to visualise the solid.
- glue the tabs in turn.

4 Find a way to place together the two half-tetrahedra to form a tetrahedron. Glue both pieces together.

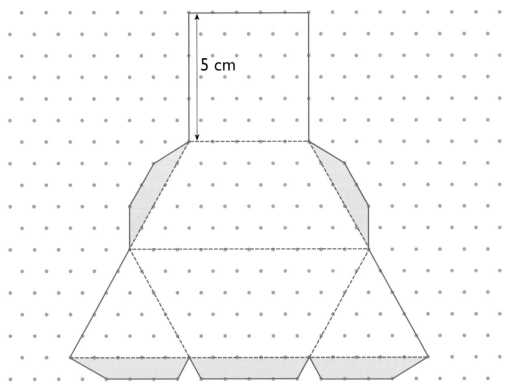

5 cm

1 Work with a partner.

Each person constructs a square-based pyramid.

● Draw a square with sides of 6 cm.
● Using your ruler and set square or protractor, draw an equilateral triangle on each side of the square.
● Add tabs to one edge of each triangle.
● Score all fold lines, cut out the net, glue the tabs in turn to form the pyramid.

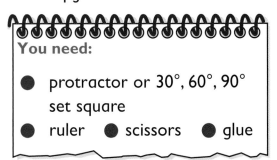

You need:

● protractor or 30°, 60°, 90° set square
● ruler ● scissors ● glue

2 Record the shapes you can make when you place both pyramids face to face in different ways.

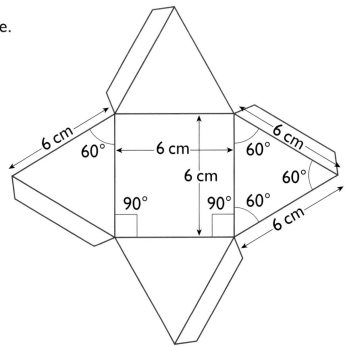

Measuring capacity

 1 Copy and complete

1 litre = ☐ ml

1 litre = ☐ cl

1 centilitre = ☐ ml

2 Write these in centilitres.

a 50 ml	b 500 ml	c 750 ml	d 1000 ml
e 80 ml	f 90 ml	g 440 ml	h 2000 ml

3 Write these in millilitres.

a 10 cl	b 100 cl	c 25 cl	d 5 cl
e 37 cl	f 98 cl	g 400 cl	h 4 cl

 1 Copy and complete the table.

Litres	Millilitres	Centilitres
1·5 l	1500 ml	150 cl
2·25 l		
3·6 l		
	3260 ml	
	5080 ml	
		75 cl
		105 cl

2 The labels show how much tea each teapot holds when full.

A

B 3¼ l

4125 ml

C 3·24 l

D 6·5 l

a Write in litres the capacity of:
   i teapots A + C
   ii teapots A + B
   iii teapots A + D

b What is the difference in capacity between:

   i teapots B and C?

   ii teapots B and D?

c How much more tea does pot D hold than pot A?

d Which teapot holds twice as much as pot B?

e What is 3 times the capacity of teapot A in litres?

f If teapot C is half full, how many centilitres of tea does it hold?

g $\frac{2}{5}$ of the tea in pot B are poured out. How many millilitres of tea does the pot still contain?

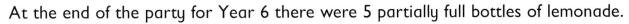

At the end of the party for Year 6 there were 5 partially full bottles of lemonade.

1 Use this information to list the 5 bottles in order of capacity, largest first.

A holds more than B.

C does not hold the least.

A does not hold the most.

E holds more than C.

Only one bottle holds less than D.

Two bottles hold more than C.

2 The measured amounts of lemonade in each bottle are:

100 cl, 75 cl, 50 cl, 25 cl and 10 cl.

Work out how much lemonade is in each bottle A to E.

Litres and millilitres

Convert smaller to larger units (e.g. ml to l) and vice versa

 1 Write the number of millilitres shown by the bold figure 6.

a 2**1**46 ml   b 3·**6** l   c 4·1**6**6 l

d 3·1**6** l   e **6**·462 l   f **6**045 ml

Example

6**1**43 ml

Answer: 6000 ml

2 Find and write the pairs of matching capacities.

Example

250 ml = 0·25 l

$\frac{3}{4}$ litre

0·8 l

5·6 l

800 ml

3·4 l

0·6 l

5600 ml

0·75 l

300 ml

3400 ml

0·3 l

600 ml

 1 Convert these litres to millilitres, then to centilitres.

a 2·5 l   b 2·25 l   c 2·050 l

d 0·52 l   e 5·02 l   f 25·0 l

Example

3.7 l = 3700 ml

= 370 cl

2 Write these millilitres as centilitres, then as litres.

a 7650 ml   b 560 ml   c 20 ml

d 5070 ml   e 700 ml   f 70 ml

Example

3420 ml = 342 cl

= 3·42 l

3 Copy and complete.

a

Amount	Rounded to nearest	
	$\frac{1}{10}$ litre	litre
2·25 l	2·3 l	2 l
3·706 l		
6·088 l		
7·990 l		

b

Amount	Rounded to nearest	
	$\frac{1}{10}$ litre	litre
530 ml	0·5 l	1 l
818 ml		
4420 ml		
690 ml		

4 Work out the answers to these in two ways.

Write your answer in millilitres.

a $\frac{1}{4}$ of 2·4 l   c $\frac{1}{2}$ of 7·6 l

b $\frac{1}{5}$ of 4·0 l   d $\frac{1}{3}$ of 5·7 l

Example

$$\frac{1}{5} \text{ of } 2·5 \text{ l}$$

$$2·5 \text{ l} ÷ 5 = 0·5 \text{ l} \qquad \frac{1}{5} \text{ of } 2500 \text{ ml}$$

$$500 \text{ ml}$$

5 Write true or false for each of these statements.

a $\frac{1}{2}$ of 3 l > $\frac{1}{4}$ of 5 l   c $\frac{3}{4}$ of 1 l > $\frac{2}{3}$ of 900 ml   e $\frac{1}{3}$ of 1·8 l > $\frac{3}{4}$ of 1200 ml

b $\frac{1}{2}$ of 1·5 l < $\frac{1}{4}$ of 2 l   d $\frac{1}{4}$ of 1 l < $\frac{1}{5}$ of 750 ml   f $\frac{4}{5}$ of 2 l < $\frac{2}{5}$ of 5000 ml

Copy and complete these patterns as far as you can go.

a

− 999 ml   − 999 ml   − 999 ml

10 l  9·001 l 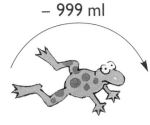 ___ l

b

− 11 cl   − 11 cl   − 11 cl

1 l  0·890 l  ___ l

What's the capacity?

- **Convert from one unit of measure to another**
- **Compare readings from different scales**

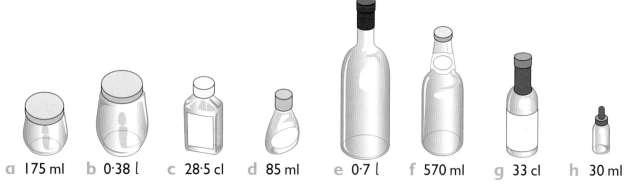

| a 175 ml | b 0·38 l | c 28·5 cl | d 85 ml | e 0·7 l | f 570 ml | g 33 cl | h 30 ml |

Use this decision tree to find which box each container belongs to.

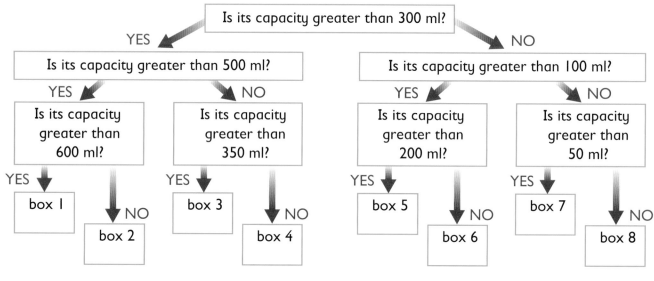

Is its capacity greater than 300 ml?

YES | NO

Is its capacity greater than 500 ml? | Is its capacity greater than 100 ml?

YES | NO | YES | NO

Is its capacity greater than 600 ml? | Is its capacity greater than 350 ml? | Is its capacity greater than 200 ml? | Is its capacity greater than 50 ml?

YES | box 1 | NO | box 2 | YES | box 3 | NO | box 4 | YES | box 5 | NO | box 6 | YES | box 7 | NO | box 8

1 For each pair of measuring jugs,

- decide which jug, A or B, contains more water.
- Find how much more water it contains.

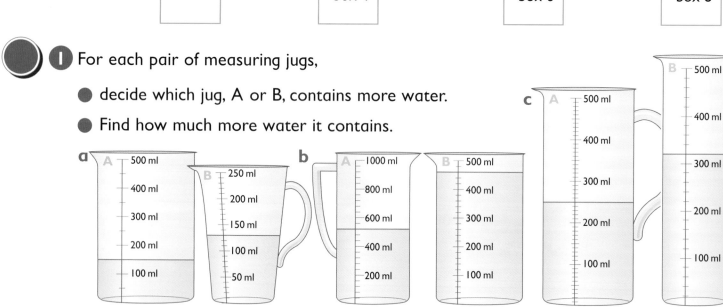

2

25 cl   0·1 l   5 cl   25 ml

You pour one or two of the above amounts of water into an empty 1 litre measuring jar.

a Show that you can make 10 different amounts.

b Find how much space will be left in the 1 litre jar each time.

3

4016 ml   2950 ml   5275 ml   3406 ml   23   47   61

Choose an amount from the measuring jar and a number from the test tube.

Divide the measuring jar amount by the test tube number.

Round your answer to one decimal place.

Professor McClitre says that there are 12 possible answers. Is she correct?

You need:
● calculator

Professor McClitre has 4 measuring jars, A, B, C and D full of liquid and 4 test tubes labelled 1, 2, 3 and 4 which are full of chemicals.

She pours the contents of one measuring jar and one test tube into an empty jug.

a How many different combinations of liquid and chemical can she make?

b What if she had a fifth test tube?

Database statistics

 1 Find the mode of these values (there may be two modes).

  a 4, 2, 6, 1, 2, 3, 8   b £42, £38, £40, £38, £42, £60

  c 300 g, 350 g, 200 g, 150 g, 200 g, 250 g, 50 g, 350 g

HINT

Mode = the most common value

2 Find the median of these values.

  a 9, 4, 4, 6, 1, 8, 3   b £210, £160, £400, £235, £92

  c 52 g, 16 g, 20 g, 83 g, 25 g, 16 g, 49 g, 85 g, 96 g

HINT

Median = the middle value when all values have been ordered smallest to largest

3 Find the mean of these values.

  a 6, 9, 6   b 8, 5, 2, 9

  c £30, £70, £25, £50, £100

  d 23 g, 41 g, 32 g, 75 g, 83 g, 25 g, 46 g, 19 g

HINT

To find the mean, find the total, then divide by the number of values.

4 Find the range of these values.

  a 20, 5, 5, 10, 60, 40, 45

  b £7, £11, £2, £2, £9, £11, £3, £6

  c 315 g, 261 g, 180 g, 592 g, 149 g, 176 g, 251 g, 832 g, 612 g, 180 g

HINT

To find the range, subtract the smallest value from the largest value.

 The database shows some information about hi-fi shops.

Shop	Cost of Crystal Hi-fi (£)	Cost of JCV Hi-fi (£)	Number of hi-fis in stock
Derrys	240	384	6
Asteroid	210	510	23
Connect	245	499	0
Tech Plus	220	377	5
Sounds	210	500	7
High Notes	260	499	5
Music World	225	500	3

You need:

● calculator

1 **a** Find the mode for each column.

b Find the range for each column.

c Find the mean for each column.

d Find the median for each column.

2 **a** Which hi-fi has the highest mode of prices?

b Which hi-fi has the lowest mean price?

c Which hi-fi has the widest range of prices? What does this mean?

3 Add this entry to the database:

Tracks	210	499	5

4 **a** Calculate the new median for each column.

b Calculate the new mode and range for each column.

c How has the median of prices of Crystal changed?

d How has the mode of prices of JCV changed?

e How do you think the mean prices have changed?

f Calculate the new mean prices. Were you correct?

1 Copy and complete the database for these packets of biscuits.

You need:
● calculator

Name of biscuit	Number of biscuits	Price	Weight
Ginger Snaps	10	85p	200 g

2 Calculate the mode, median, mean and range for each column in your table.

 **Ginger Snaps** 10 biscuits 85p 200 g

 **Cream Sandwich** 20 biscuits £1·12 500 g

 **Butter Wheels** 8 biscuits £1 90 g

Coconut Swirls 12 biscuits 70p 160 g

 **Strawberry Hearts** 15 biscuits 96p 300 g

 **Fruit Bars** 12 biscuits £1·42 180 g

 **Chocolate Fingers** 10 biscuits £1·20 90 g

 **LEMON DROPS** 10 biscuits 75p 200 g

 **Cherry Spots** 20 biscuits £2·35 700 g

Conversion graphs

 I Copy and complete this table.

kilograms (kg)	pounds (lb)
0	0
I	2
2	
3	
4	
5	
6	
7	
8	

2 Use your table to complete this graph.

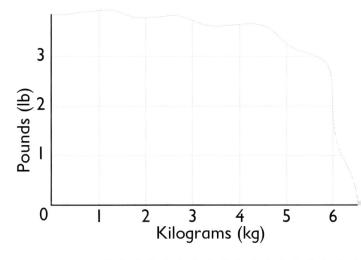

Use your graph to answer these questions.

3 Convert these weights to pounds.

  a 2·5 kg   b 7·5 kg   c I·5 kg   d 4·5 kg

4 Convert these weights to kilograms.

  a II lb   b I lb   c I3 lb   d 7 lb

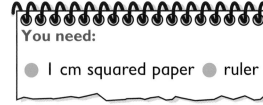

You need:

● I cm squared paper ● ruler

Remember

I kg ≈ 2 lb

 This graph converts between gallons and litres. Use it to estimate the answer to these questions.

I Convert these to litres.

  a 6 gallons

  b I4 gallons

  c 5 gallons

  d I7 gallons

You need:

● graph paper
● ruler

Remember

2 gallons is about 9 litres.

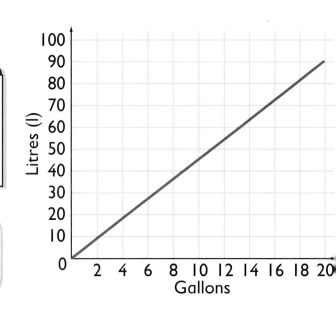

2 Convert these to gallons.

   a 90 litres   **b** 30 litres   **c** 70 litres   **d** 20 litres

3 Copy and complete this table of values.

Gallons	Litres (l)
0	0
2	9
4	18
6	
8	
10	

4 Use your table to draw a conversion graph on graph paper.

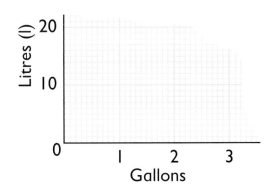

Use your graph to answer these questions.

5 How many litres does each drum contain?

   a 5 gallons   **b** 9 gallons   **c** 1·4 gallons   **d** 7·8 gallons

6 How many gallons does each drum contain?

   a 15 litres   **b** 40 litres   **c** 28 litres   **d** 34 litres

---

1 1 kg is almost exactly 2·2 lb. Copy and complete the table.
Use your calculator if necessary.

kilograms (kg)	0	10	20	30	40	50	60	70	80
pounds (lb)									

2 Use your table to draw a conversion graph.
Use these scales for the axes: horizontal axis 2 cm to 10 kg; vertical axis 2 cm to 20 lb.
Then use your graph to answer the following questions.

3 Convert these weights to pounds.

   a 25 kg   **b** 17 kg   **c** 62 kg   **d** 43 kg

4 Convert these weights to kilograms.

   a 120 lb   **b** 36 lb   **c** 94 lb   **d** 142 lb

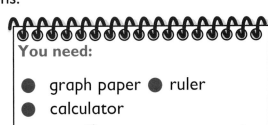

You need:
- graph paper ● ruler
- calculator

Nature pie charts

 The pie chart shows the animals a vet saw in a week.

Animal	Percentage
Cats	
Dogs	
Hamsters and Rabbits	
Others	

Animals seen by vet

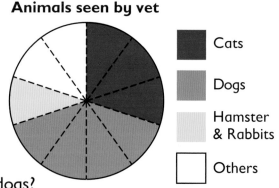

■ Cats
■ Dogs
▨ Hamster & Rabbits
□ Others

a Copy and complete the table. Do not use a calculator.

b What percentage of the animals are cats and dogs?

c What percentage of the animals are hamsters, rabbits and dogs?

d What percentage of the animals are not dogs?

2 The pie chart shows the animals in a sanctuary.

a Make a table of percentages.

b What percentage of the animals are donkeys and horses?

c What percentage of the animals are not horses?

d What percentage of the animals are not donkeys or horses?

Sanctuary animals

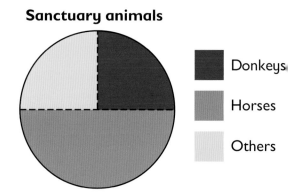

■ Donkeys
■ Horses
▨ Others

 The pie charts show the fish in three tanks.

Ben's fish tank
Larry's fish tank
Gurjit's fish tank

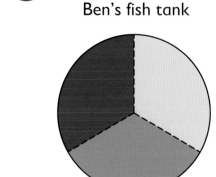
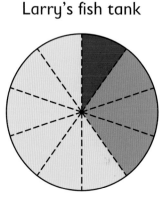
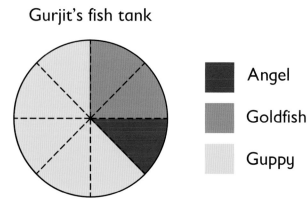

■ Angel
■ Goldfish
□ Guppy

1 Make a table of percentages for each fish tank.

2 **a** Whose tank has the greatest percentage of Guppy fish?

b Whose tank has the greatest percentage of Goldfish?

c Whose tank has the least percentage of Angel fish?

d What percentage of Gurjit's fish are Guppy and Angel?

e What percentage of Ben's fish are Goldfish and Angel?

f Whose fish tank has the highest percentage of Angel and Guppy fish?

3 The pie chart shows the animals on a farm.

a Make a table of percentages.

b What percentage of the animals are cows and sheep?

c What percentage of the animals are not cows?

d What is the percentage difference between chickens and sheep?

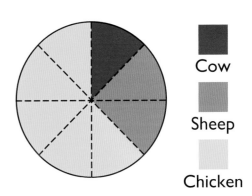

Cow

Sheep

Chicken

The pie charts show the birds that visit three gardens.

1 Estimate the percentage of each type of bird. Make a table for each pie chart. Your percentages must add up to 100%.

2 Write a paragraph comparing the type of birds that visit the three gardens.

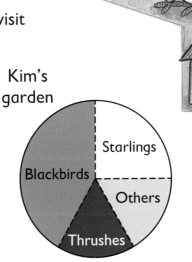

Myrna's garden

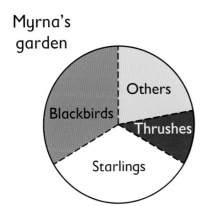

Blackbirds

Others

Thrushes

Starlings

Wayne's garden

Thrushes

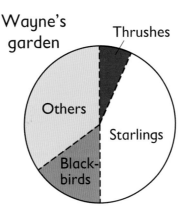

Others

Starlings

Black-birds

Kim's garden

Blackbirds

Starlings

Others

Thrushes

People pie charts

The pie charts show the sizes of families in two districts. Copy and complete the tables.

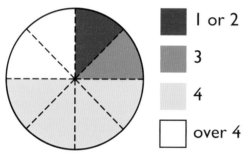

Templeton Estate
Number of families: 48

- 1 or 2
- 3
- 4
- over 4

Size of family	Number
1 or 2	
3	
4	
over 4	

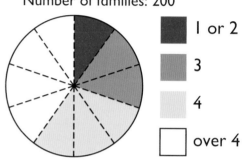

Sidburg Estate
Number of families: 200

- 1 or 2
- 3
- 4
- over 4

Size of family	Number
1 or 2	
3	
4	
over 4	

1 The pie charts show the ages of residents of two hotels.

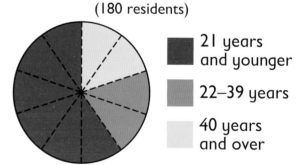

Miranda hotel residents
(300 residents)

- 21 years and younger
- 22–39 years
- 40 years and over

Age	Number	Percentage (%)
21 years and younger		
22–39		
40 and over		

Compton hotel residents
(180 residents)

- 21 years and younger
- 22–39 years
- 40 years and over

Age	Number	Percentage (%)
21 years and younger		
22–39		
40 and over		

a Copy and complete the tables.

b Which do you think is the family hotel? Explain why.

c What percentage of residents staying at the Miranda hotel are over 21 years old?

d What percentage of residents staying at the Compton hotel are under 40 years old?

2 The pie charts show the employees of a bus station and a drinks factory. Make a table for each pie chart.

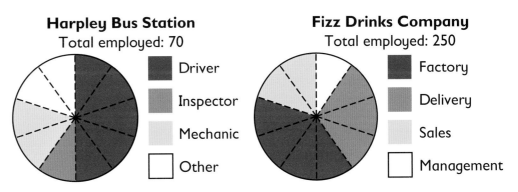

Harpley Bus Station
Total employed: 70

Driver
Inspector
Mechanic
Other

Fizz Drinks Company
Total employed: 250

Factory
Delivery
Sales
Management

3 The pie chart shows the staff of an airline. There are 12 receptionists.

a How many pilots are there?

b How many stewards are there?

c How many other staff are there?

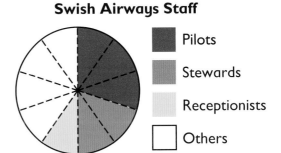

Swish Airways Staff

Pilots
Stewards
Receptionists
Others

The tables shows the ages of club members. Draw a pie chart for each table. Colour the sectors and make a key.

Heathley Cricket Club

Age	Percentage (%)
Under 20	20
20–39	30
40–59	40
60 and over	10

Binkford Bowling club

Age	Percentage (%)
Under 20	30
20–39	40
40–59	15
60 and over	15

Smallbridge Chess Club

Age	Percentage (%)
Under 20	15
20–39	30
40–59	25
60 and over	30

You need:
● RCM 18: Percentage pie charts
● coloured pencils

Results pie and bar charts

● **Represent data in different ways and understand its meaning**

 Gary played a computer game lots of times. The pie chart shows his scores.

Gary's results

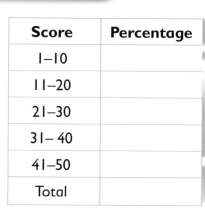

Score	Percentage
1–10	
11–20	
21–30	
31–40	
41–50	
Total	

1 Copy the table.

2 a In what percentage of the games did he score above 10?

b In what percentage of the games did he score below 21?

c In what percentage of the games did he score above 20?

d In what percentage of the games did he score between 11 and 30?

e Which scores are the most common?

3 Copy and complete the percentage bar chart.

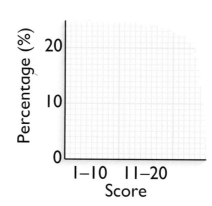

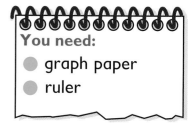
You need:
● graph paper
● ruler

 80 children in Year 6 took a science test. The test was out of 25 marks. The pie chart shows their results.

Science test results

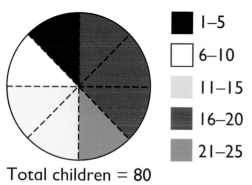

Total children = 80

Score	Number of children	Percentage
1–5		
6–10		
11–15		
16–20		
21–25		
Total		

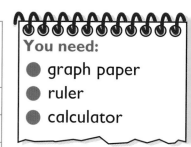
You need:
● graph paper
● ruler
● calculator

1 Copy and complete the table.

2 a What percentage of the children scored fewer than 11 marks?

  b What percentage of the children scored 11 or more marks?

  c What percentage of the children scored between 11 and 20 marks?

  d What percentage of the children scored between 6 and 15 marks?

  e Which scores are the most common?

3 Copy and complete this bar chart.

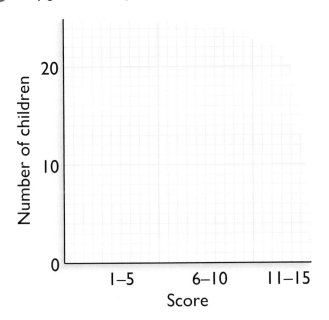

4 This pie chart shows the history results for Year 6.

  a Make a table like the one on page 68.

  b Write three sentences comparing the science and history results.

History test results

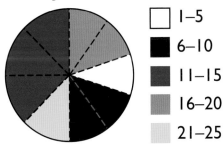

☐	1–5
■	6–10
■	11–15
■	16–20
☐	21–25

Total children = 240

The bar chart shows the runs scored by batsmen during a large regional cricket tournament.

1 Copy and complete the table.

2 Draw a pie chart to show the scores.

You need:
● RCM 18: Percentage pie charts
● calculator   ● ruler

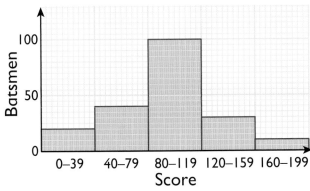

Score	Number of batsmen	Percentage (%)
0–39		
40–79		
80–119		
120–159		
160–199		

3 Which type of chart do you think represents the data best? Why?

Experimental percentages

● **Represent data in different ways and understand its meaning**

 Work in pairs.

1. Take turns to roll the dice. Add 1 to each number.

   Find the product of these numbers. Do this 50 times.

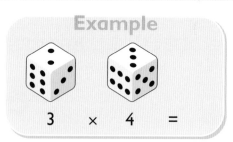

Example

$3 \quad \times \quad 4 \quad =$

You need:

● two 1-6 dice

2. Record your results in this tally chart.

   Before you begin, predict which class will have the most tally marks.

3. Calculate the total frequency.

4. Was your prediction correct?

Product	Tally	Frequency
0 –9		
10 –19		
20 –29		
30 –39		
40 – 49		
Total frequency		

 Work in pairs.

1. Shuffle the dominoes and lay them face down. Choose a domino each.

   Add the dots of both dominoes.

   Do this 50 times.

The total is 11

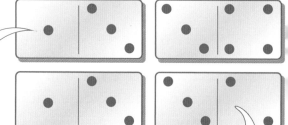

The total is 9

2. Record your results in this tally chart.

   Before you begin, predict which class will have the most tally marks.

Total	Tally	Frequency	Percentage
0 – 4			
5 – 9			
10 –14			
15 –19			
20 –24			
	Total frequency		

You need:

● set of dominoes
● graph paper
● ruler

3 a Calculate the total frequency.

  b Convert the frequencies to percentages.

4 a Which totals are the most common?

  b What percentage of totals are less than 10?

  c What percentage of totals are 15 or more?

  d What percentage of totals lie between 10 and 19?

5 Copy and complete the percentage bar chart.

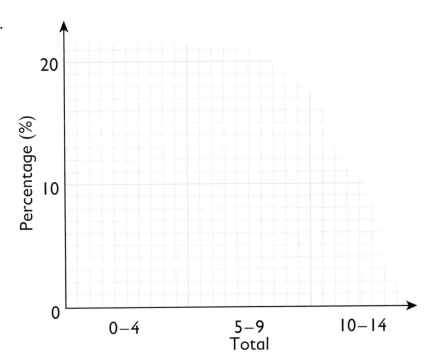

Work in pairs.

1 Roll five dice each. Add the numbers together. Do this 50 times.

2 Make a tally chart for your results. Decide the classes you will need. Before you begin, predict the class that will have the most totals.

Total	Tally	Frequency	Percentage
	Total frequency		

3 Convert the frequencies to percentages.

4 a Was your prediction correct?

  b What percentage of totals are less than 20?

  c What percentage of totals are 10 or more?

5 Draw a bar chart for the data.

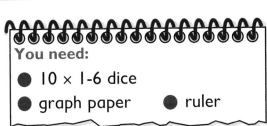

You need:
● 10 × 1-6 dice
● graph paper   ● ruler

What's next?

1. Work with a partner. Shuffle a pack of 1-10 number cards. Place them face down.

2. Use the words on the right to answer the following questions.

   a What is the chance of turning up an even number?

   b What is the chance of a number less than 2?

no chance   even chance

impossible   unlikely

likely   small chance

certain   good chance

You need:
● a set of 1-10 number cards

3. Take turns to turn over the top card of the pack until all the cards have been revealed. Repeat question 2 each time.

1. Work with a partner. Each person draws two 5 × 5 grids as their Battleship game board.

   You need:
   ● 1-6 die   ● ruler
   ● paper and pencil

2. Place your Battleships, Submarines and Destroyers on your grid using letters B, S and D. Conceal your board from your opponent.

3. Take turns to roll the die twice each.

   The first number gives the column; the second gives the row of your target square. Ignore a 6.

   Your opponent will tell you if you have a miss or a hit, and what you have hit.

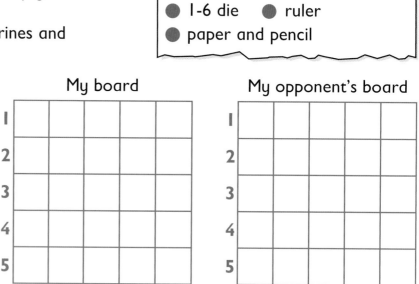

4 Enter your shot on your opponent's grid, using a **✗** for a miss, and the letters B, D or S for a hit.

5 Before each roll of the dice, complete one of the following statements, starting with **a**. Choose a different statement each time. The other player checks the statement.

a _____ is unlikely

b _____ and _____ are equally likely

c _____ has an even chance

d _____ is impossible

e _____ is less likely than _____

My board

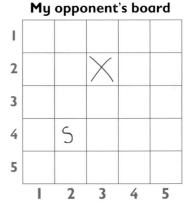

My opponent's board

	1	2	3
1	B	S	D
2	S		B		B
3	D		D
4	B		B	S
5	S	✗		D	B

| | 1 | 2 | 3 | 4 | 5 |

Example

A miss is likely.

Battleships and Submarines are equally likely.

6 Continue playing until all of one player's vessels are sunk.

Work with a partner.

1 Remove the picture cards from a pack of playing cards. Shuffle the pack and place it face down.

2 Take turns to remove one card at a time, placing it in one of four columns according to its suit.

3 Before each turn, complete one of the following statements starting with **a**. Choose a different statement each time. The other person checks the statement.

a _____ is unlikely

b _____ and _____ are equally likely

c _____ has an even chance

d _____ is impossible

e _____ is less likely than _____

You need:

● a pack of playing cards

Example

Clubs are unlikely.

Even numbers are less likely than odd numbers.

Timing problems

 1 Copy and complete this table of cooking times.

Cooking time in minutes	Weight in kilograms						
	0·5	1	1·5	2	2·5	3	3·5
Lamb	30	60					
Chicken	20	40					

COOKING TIMES

Lamb
30 minutes for every 0·5 kg

Chicken
20 minutes for every 0·5 kg

2 Jean is roasting a 2·5 kg chicken. She puts it into the oven at 4:00 p.m. At what time will the chicken be ready to eat?

3 Robbie roasted a rack of lamb in his oven. It took 2 hours to cook. What weight of lamb did he roast?

A restaurant chef uses these roasting times for meat and poultry.

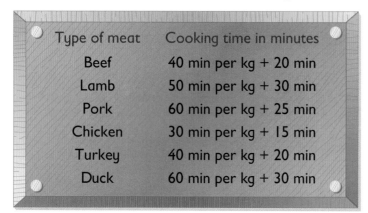

Type of meat	Cooking time in minutes
Beef	40 min per kg + 20 min
Lamb	50 min per kg + 30 min
Pork	60 min per kg + 25 min
Chicken	30 min per kg + 15 min
Turkey	40 min per kg + 20 min
Duck	60 min per kg + 30 min

Example

Cooking time for 2·5 kg beef

$(40 \text{ min} \times 2·5) + 20 \text{ min}$ = 100 min + 20 min

= 120 min

= 2 hours

1 Find the cooking time in minutes, then in hours and minutes for these:

a beef 4 kg    b lamb 3·5 kg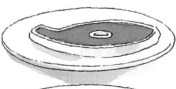

c pork 3 kg   d chicken 2·5 kg

e turkey 4 kg

f duck 2·5 kg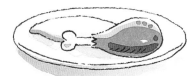

2 The restaurant carvery opens at 5:00 p.m. Work out when the chef must put these meats into the ovens so that they are ready to serve at 5:00 p.m.

Copy and complete this table.

Type of meat	Weight of meat	Roasting time in oven in minutes	Time meat is put into oven
Beef	6 kg		
Lamb	5 kg		
Pork	4·5 kg		
Chicken	5 kg		
Turkey	6 kg		
Duck	4 kg		

The chef drew up this 'ready reckoner' for roasting beef.

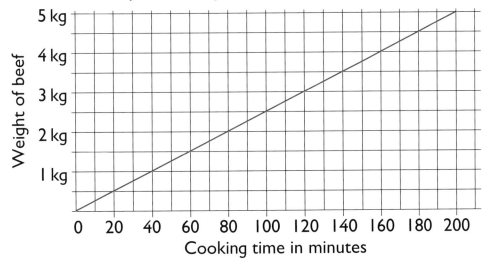

You need:
- graph paper or squared paper
- ruler

(add 20 minutes to end of cooking time)

Using the graph he worked out that 3 kg of beef needed 120 minutes plus 20 minutes, or 2 hours 20 minutes to cook.

1 Draw up similar graphs for the other meats on the previous page.

2 Use the graphs to work out the cooking time for 3 kg weights of each meat.

Remember to add the extra minutes to the end of the cooking time.

Litres, pints and gallons

- Know imperial units (pint, gallon)
- Know rough equivalents of litres and pints or gallons

Use the graph to answer these questions.

1 Approximately how many pints are there in:

  a 4 litres?

  b $4\frac{1}{2}$ litres?

  c $2\frac{1}{2}$ litres?

  d 2 litres?

2 Approximately how many litres and tenths of a litre are there in:

  a 1 pint?

  b $2\frac{1}{2}$ pints?

  c $6\frac{1}{4}$ pints?

  d 8 pints?

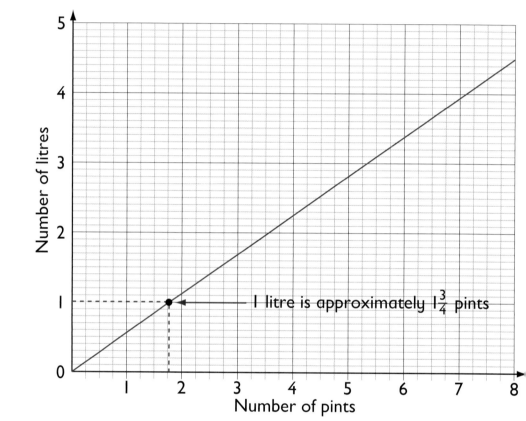

I litre is approximately $1\frac{3}{4}$ pints

You will find the scale on the next page beside the petrol pumps in filling stations and garages.

Use the scale to answer these questions.

Remember

4·5 litres = 1 gallon or 8 pints

1 litre = $1\frac{3}{4}$ pints

1 Write your answer to the nearest litre.

Approximately how many litres are there in:

  a 2 gallons?   b 3 gallons?   c 4 gallons?

  d 8 gallons?   e 0·9 gallons?   f 1·8 gallons?

2 Write your answer to one decimal place.

Approximately how many gallons are there in:

a 7 litres?　　　　**b** 10 litres?　　　**c** 14 litres?

d 45 litres?　　　　**e** 22 litres?　　　**f** 27 litres?

3 A milkman has 120 houses on his round.

He delivers 1 pint of milk to $\frac{1}{4}$ of the houses
and 2 pints to $\frac{1}{2}$ of the houses.

The rest of his customers take 3 pints of milk.

Work out the quantity of milk he delivers each day:

a in pints

b in gallons

c in litres

4 The milkman's order for
the local primary school is
45 litres of milk per week.

How many pints of milk
does the milkman deliver to
the school each day?

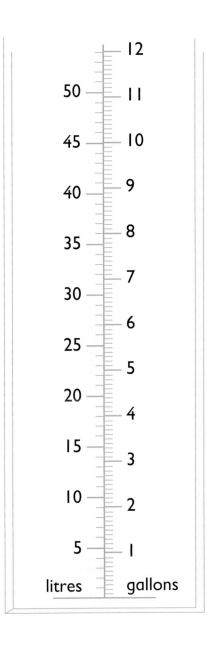

The petrol tank capacities for these super minis are:

Fiat Punto　　　10·3 gallons

Ford Fiesta　　　8·8 gallons

Rover 25　　　　11·0 gallons

Toyota Yaris　　9·7 gallons

VW Polo　　　　9·8 gallons

Using the scale above, work out how many litres,
to the nearest litre, there are in a full tank of petrol for each car.

Marine centre problems

A goldfish needs 9 litres of water.

1 Work out how many goldfish you can keep in tanks which have these capacities.

a   90 litres
b   45 litres

c   108 litres
d   450 litres

> **Example**
>
> 27 litres in tank.
> Number of goldfish = 27 ÷ 9
> = 3 goldfish

2 You want to stock some tanks with goldfish.

Work out the capacity of the tank you need for these numbers of goldfish.

> **Example**
>
> 1 goldfish needs 9 litres
> For 6 goldfish = (6 × 9) litres
> = 54 litres

a   4 goldfish
b   8 goldfish
c   20 goldfish
d   100 goldfish

 Kevin's job is to refuel the boats.

He completes these columns in his record book for each sale.

Name of boat	Meter reading in litres		
	before refuelling	after refuelling	litres sold
Sea Hawk	7326 l	7430 l	104 l
Sea Urchin	7430 l	7665 l	
Sea Eagle	7665 l		269 l
Sea Farer		8481 l	547 l

1 Work out the missing entries in Kevin's record book for the Sea Urchin, Sea Eagle and Sea Farer.

2 The ferry to the island has two fuel tanks.

   a How much fuel altogether is in the ferry's tanks?

   b How much more fuel is in tank 1 than tank 2?

   c The captain draws alongside to refuel.

     The ferry needs 4500 litres altogether for the day's ferry crossings.

     Work out how many litres of fuel are added to Tank 1 and Tank 2 so that each tank holds the same amount.

Tank 1
1095 l

Tank 2
876 l

3 The large marine aquarium is stocked with 25 fish, each fish having approximately 18 litres of water. What is the capacity, in litres, of the aquarium?

For water
1 ml = 1 g
1000 ml = 1000 g

The training pool for young children holds 80 000 litres of water.

1 Using the information above, find the weight, in kilograms, of water in the pool.

2 Chemicals are added to the water in the pool at regular intervals.

If 500 ml of chemicals are needed for every 10 000 litres, how many litres of chemicals have to be added to the water?

Calculating areas

using 2 triangles	using 3 triangles	using 4 triangles

  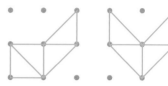

area = 1 cm²   area = 1$\frac{1}{2}$ cm²   area = 2 cm²

1 Use the four triangles to make the above shapes.
Then record your answers on 1 cm square dot paper.

You need:
- 4 identical right-angled triangles
- 1 cm square dot paper

a Take 2 triangles. Find 1 more shape with an area of 1 cm².

b Take 3 triangles. Find 2 more shapes which have areas of 1$\frac{1}{2}$ cm².

c Take 4 triangles. Find 8 more shapes with areas of 2 cm².

2 a Draw 3 different shapes which are made by joining 5 right-angled triangles.

b Work out the area of each shape.

1 Work out the area of the red shapes.

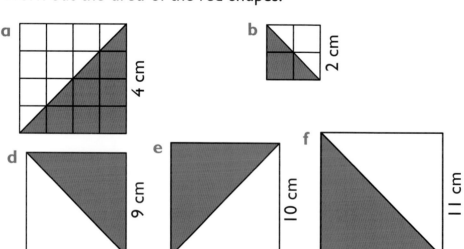

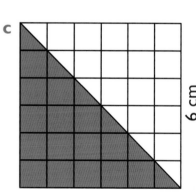

a 4 cm

b 2 cm

c 6 cm

d 9 cm, 9 cm

e 10 cm, 10 cm

f 11 cm, 11 cm

2 Change each right-angled triangle into a square and find the area of the triangle.

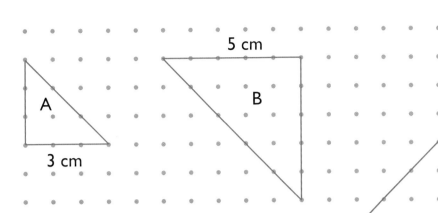

5 cm

A

3 cm

B

7 cm

C

3 Find the area of the tangram square.

4 Find the area of these tangram pieces:

a triangle A + triangle B

b triangle A

c triangle C

d triangle G

e square F

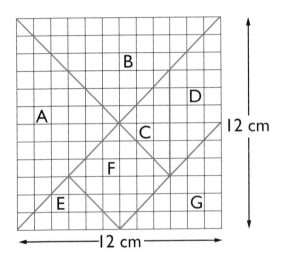

12 cm

12 cm

These shapes all have 8 pins on their perimeter. Some have no pins inside, some have one pin and some, two or more.

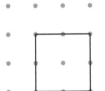   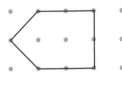

You need:

● 1 cm square dot paper

1 On 1 cm square dot paper, make different shapes which have 8 pins on their perimeter. Copy and complete the table.

Number of pins inside (P)	0	1	2	3	4	5
Area in cm² (A)	3					

2 Predict the area of shapes with 6 and 10 pins inside. Make a general statement about the relationship between the number of pins inside a shape and its area.

Areas of right-angled triangles

① Work out the area of each triangle.

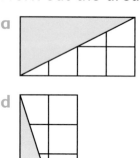 a

b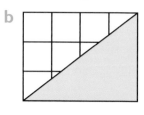

c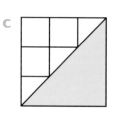

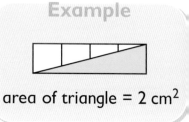
d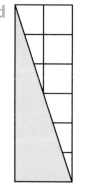

e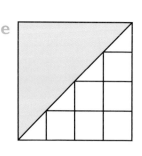

f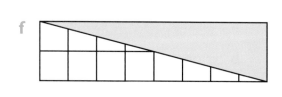

② Write the letter of the triangle which has the same area as:

   a triangle b   b   triangle e

① Calculate the areas of these right-angled triangles.

You need:

● 1 cm squared paper
● ruler   ● scissors
● glue

a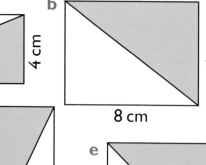
10 cm

b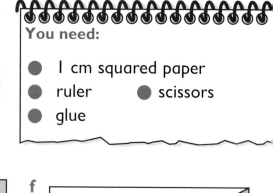
4 cm
8 cm
6 cm

c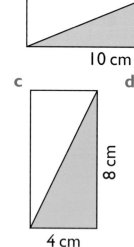
8 cm
4 cm

d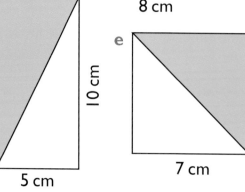
10 cm
5 cm

e
7 cm
7 cm

f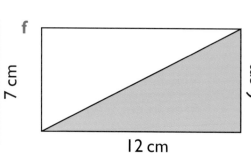
12 cm
6 cm

82

2 **a** Copy each triangle below on to 1 cm squared paper and cut it out.

b Transform the triangle into a rectangle and paste it into your exercise book.

c Find the area of the transformed shape.

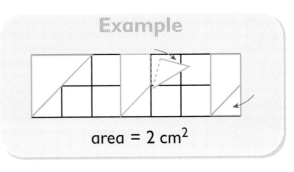

Example

area = 2 cm²

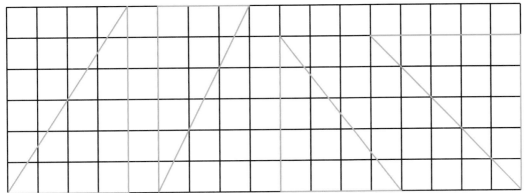

3 On 1 cm squared paper, draw two different right-angled triangles which have an area of 10 cm².

 Copy each pentagon on to 1 cm squared paper.
Now find a way to work out the area of each pentagon.

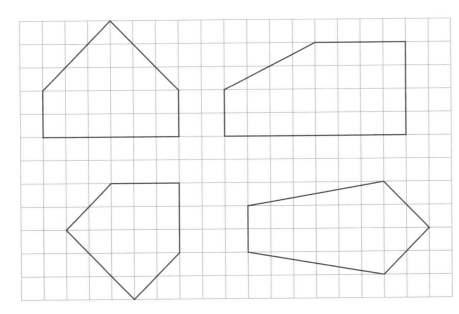

You need:

● 1 cm squared paper
● ruler

HINT

Decide where to draw lines to divide the pentagon into rectangles and triangles.

World times

● **Read and interpret scales as accurately as the problem requires**

Use the world time chart to help you.

① It is 12:00 in London.

Write the time it is in these cities in two ways:

a Athens   c Calcutta   e Houston   g Tokyo

b Denver   d Perth   f Rio de Janeiro   h Oslo

> **Example**
>
> Mumbai   17:00   5 p.m.

② Name a city which is:

a 2 hours ahead of London   d 8 hours behind London

b 5 hours behind London   e 7 hours behind London

c 9 hours ahead of London   f 10 hours ahead of London

> **Example**
>
> 6 hours ahead of London
>
> London + 6 hours is Calcutta

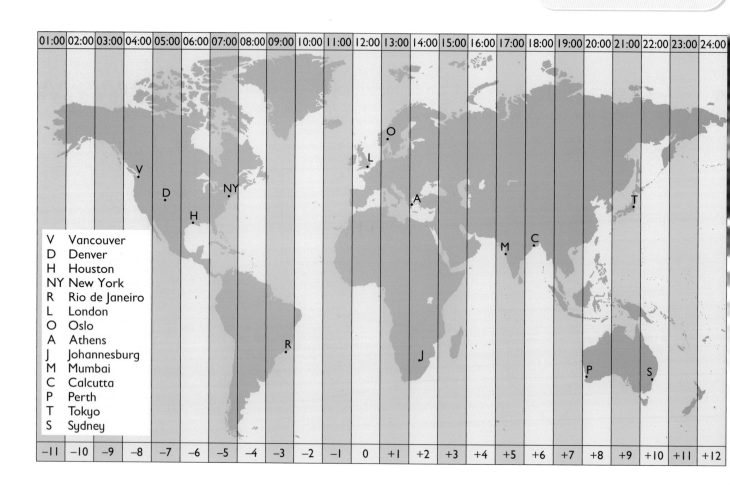

01:00	02:00	03:00	04:00	05:00	06:00	07:00	08:00	09:00	10:00	11:00	12:00	13:00	14:00	15:00	16:00	17:00	18:00	19:00	20:00	21:00	22:00	23:00	24:00

V Vancouver
D Denver
H Houston
NY New York
R Rio de Janeiro
L London
O Oslo
A Athens
J Johannesburg
M Mumbai
C Calcutta
P Perth
T Tokyo
S Sydney

−11	−10	−9	−8	−7	−6	−5	−4	−3	−2	−1	0	+1	+2	+3	+4	+5	+6	+7	+8	+9	+10	+11	+12

1 It is 12 noon in London. In which city is the time:

a 6 a.m.   b 21:00   c 04:00   d 10 p.m.

2 Write the time differences in hours between these cities:

a New York and Athens   c Vancouver and Oslo

b Rio de Janeiro and Perth   d Denver and Johannesburg

3 It is 8:30 p.m. in Athens. Write the time it is in:

a London   c Calcutta

b Houston   d Tokyo

4 It is 04:15 Saturday in Sydney. What is the time and day in:

a Calcutta   b London   c New York   d Perth

5 Your flight for Vancouver leaves Tokyo at 12:00 on a Thursday.
What day is it in Vancouver?

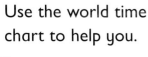

Use the world time chart to help you.

Key

B   Banff
C   Chicago
D   Denver
H   Houston
M   Miami
NY   New York
S   Seattle
SF   San Francisco
T   Toronto

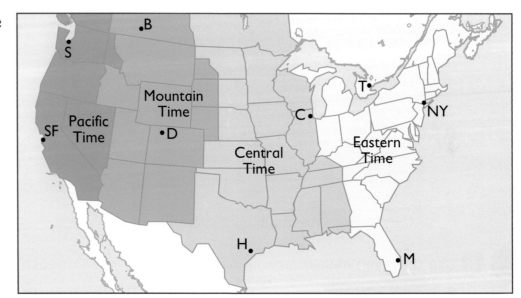

Choose a city in each time zone to set up offices for your computer company.

1 Your London head office works from 09:00 to 17:00.

Write the times during which each of your American offices can phone London.

2 In the USA, work begins at 7:30 a.m. It is cheaper to phone America after 12:00.

Draw up a list of phone times for when the London head office can phone each American office at the cheaper rate.

Areas of nets

Henri collects newspaper cuttings about his favourite football team and pastes them in his scrapbook. Find the area of each newspaper cutting.

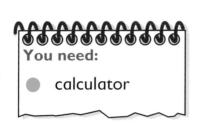

You need:
● calculator

Example

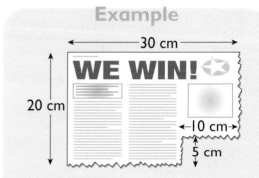

Area of page = (20 × 30) cm²
= 600 cm²

Area cut out = (10 × 5) cm²
= 50 cm²

Area of cutting = (600 − 50) cm²
= 550 cm²

a
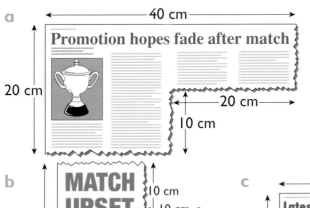

b **c** **d**
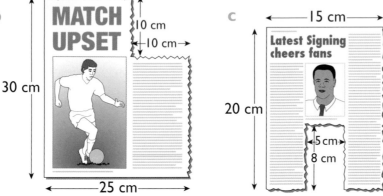

 1 Use the given measurements to calculate the area of each net.

a
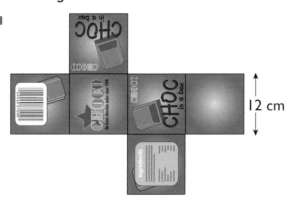

b
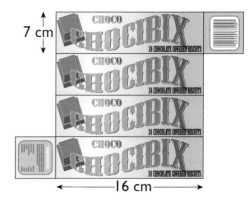

2 Find the difference in surface area of the nets.

3 7 tabs, each 1 cm wide, are added to the net to make a box.
Find the total area of paper needed for the box.

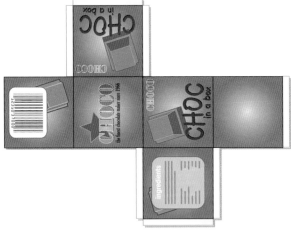

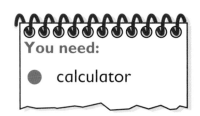

You need:
● calculator

Now where did I put
my calculator?

4 Rory's gran keeps family photographs in an old box.
The box is an open-topped cube with sides of 9 inches.
Use the fact that 1 inch ≈ 2·5 cm to find the surface
area of Gran's box in square centimetres.

Nafissa has four sheets of card.

She is about to make the net for the cube in question **3** of the ⬤ activity.

Which sheet of card would be her best choice?

Explain your reason.

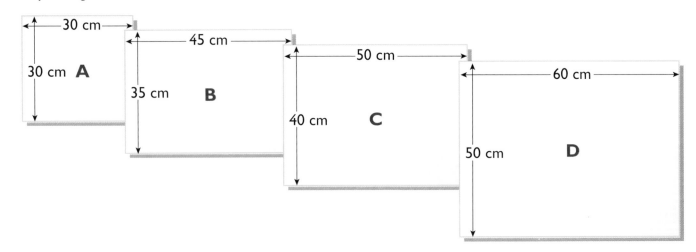

Calculations check-out

● Use approximations and inverse operations to estimate and check

Work out the calculations and then check them using the suggested method.

1 Check these calculations by adding the numbers in a different order.

a	31 + 25 + 51	e	75 + 36 + 15	i	13 + 20 + 46 + 53
b	74 + 38 + 20	f	73 + 61 + 30	j	19 + 64 + 38 + 22
c	61 + 53 + 87	g	12 + 36 + 59 + 84	k	21 + 48 + 16 + 34
d	55 + 39 + 48	h	32 + 52 + 16 + 62	l	37 + 52 + 18 + 26

2 Check these calculations by using the odd and even rules.

a	48 + 63	e	486 − 201	i	152 + 364
b	47 + 25	f	255 + 320	j	271 + 632
c	84 − 26	g	420 + 380	k	286 − 42
d	40 − 27	h	163 − 90	l	437 + 193

3 Check these calculations by working out the inverse operation.

You may use a calculator.

a	4885 + 3621	e	6985 + 3210	i	6914 − 3823
b	8542 + 2704	f	9862 − 3521	j	9621 − 3541
c	7514 + 1397	g	5412 − 4213	k	5861 − 4213
d	7852 + 5793	h	4125 − 3781	l	7061 − 3469

For each of the calculations below:

● make an estimate of the answer.

● work out the answer.

● choose a checking method.

● write the calculation you did to check your answer.

You need:

● calculator

You may want to record what you do in a table similar to the following.

	Calculation	Estimate	Answer	Checking method	Checking calculation
a	4826 + 3941	9000	8767	inverse (calculator)	8767 − 4826 = 3941
b	25 + 17 + 39 + 29	100	110	mentally	25 + 17 + 39 + 29 = 110

a 4826 + 3941

b 25 + 17 + 39 + 29

c 632 + 152

d 7965 + 2391

e 635 + 198

f 8463 − 7963

g 960 − 352

h 14 + 25 + 36 + 98

i 78 263 − 6354

j 32 + 65 + 75 + 10

k 963 + 472

l 36 421 + 95 200

m 63 + 35 + 14 + 37

n 674 − 350

o 7514 − 3000

p 6800 − 2600

q 8400 + 6100

r 84 + 69

s 6952 − 3841

t 75 320 + 52 100

u 9642 + 6300

v 7500 − 2510

w 82 + 63 + 41 + 37

x 63 140 − 23 400

Check these calculations to see if they are correct.
Write down the method you use.

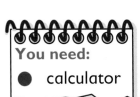

You need:

● calculator

a 4536 + 8951 = 13 487

b 7861 − 3524 = 4347

c 15 + 36 + 94 + 82 + 67 = 295

d 45 362 − 28 692 = 16 670

e 23 855 + 14 869 = 38 624

f 6300 + 5800 + 9100 = 21 230

g 78 330 + 78 251 = 156 581

h 89 + 62 + 37 + 15 + 96 = 299

i 8563 + 6941 + 2871 = 18 365

j 48 362 − 25 032 = 73 394

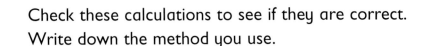

89

Pizza pizza

PIZZAS	small	large
Mushroom	£4.70	£7.95
Tuna	£5.90	£8.55
Pepperoni	£6.35	£
Chicken	£	£8.10
Extra cheese 75p		

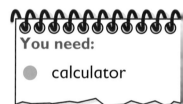

Solve these word problems. Show all your working out.
You can use a calculator if it is the most appropriate method.

You need:
● calculator

a   I buy a small pepperoni pizza with extra cheese.
   How much does it cost me?

b   I pay for my small pepperoni pizza with extra cheese on
   with a £10 note. How much change do I get?

c   I buy a large tuna pizza and a large chicken pizza.
   How much do I spend?

d   I buy 2 small tuna pizzas and pay with a £20 note.
   How much change do I get?

e   On Wednesday evenings the pizzas are half price.
   I buy 4 large chicken pizzas. How much do I pay?

f   There is a special offer: Buy 3 pizzas and get the
   cheapest one free! I buy a large mushroom, tuna
   and chicken pizza. How much do I pay?

Solve these word problems. Show all your working out.
You can use a calculator if it is the most appropriate method.

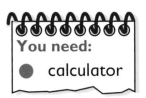

You need:
● calculator

a   I buy a small chicken pizza and a large tuna pizza. The total cost is £15.95. What is the cost of the small chicken pizza?

b   I buy 3 small tuna pizzas and 3 large pepperoni pizzas. I pay with a £50 note and get £6.35 change. What is the price of one large pepperoni pizza?

c   I buy two large pepperoni pizzas. I pay with a £20 note. How much change do I get?

d   I buy one of every small pizza, and have extra cheese on two of them. How much do I pay?

e   I buy 2 small pizzas the same and one different large pizza. The cost is £17.50. Which three pizzas did I get?

f   Large chicken pizzas are reduced by 10%. I buy 4. How much is the total cost?

The pizza seller decides to start charging per slice of pizza. He is going to cut each pizza into 6 slices. How much should he charge per slice? If he rounds up the prices, how much extra will he be making per pizza?

You need:
● calculator

Running times

● Solve multi-step problems and choose and use appropriate calculation strategies including calculator use

School Running Team Times for 1 km

Maria	438·29 secs
George	476·04 secs
Ikram	515·21 secs
Julia	463·57 secs
Suraya	502·96 secs
Jacob	489·37 secs

Solve each of the word problems.
Show all your working out.

a Put everyone's times in order from slowest to fastest.

b What is the total time for Maria and Ikram?

c What is the difference between Suraya's time and Julia's time?

d Jacob and another of his friends add their times together. They come to 896·15. What is his friend's time?

e The team coach says 'I want everyone to improve their time by 10 seconds.' What is everyone's target time?

f What is the total time of the three fastest members of the team?

Solve each of the word problems.
Show all your working out.

a What is the difference between the fastest
time and the slowest time?

b What is the total time for the girls?

c What is the total time for the boys?

d Who are faster, boys or girls?
What is the difference between the
boys' time and the girls' time?

e The team's time is added to another
team's time and the total time is 4873·57.
What was the other team's time?

f Sam joins the team and his time is added
to the total. The new team time is
3380·72. What is Sam's time?

You can use a calculator for these questions.

a What is everyone's time in minutes?

b What is everyone's time in hours?

c What is the average team time?

d If everyone's performance improved by 5%, what would the new team time be?

e Compare your answer for question d with a friend. Have you got the same answer?
If not, why do you think this is?

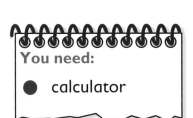

You need:

● calculator

Problem fractions

● Solve problems involving fractions

 1 Put these fractions in order, smallest to largest.

a $\dfrac{2}{5}, \dfrac{4}{10}, \dfrac{1}{3}$ b $\dfrac{1}{2}, \dfrac{2}{6}, \dfrac{1}{3}$ c $\dfrac{5}{8}, \dfrac{1}{2}, \dfrac{1}{4}$

d $\dfrac{7}{10}, \dfrac{2}{5}, \dfrac{3}{4}$ e $\dfrac{5}{9}, \dfrac{13}{18}, \dfrac{2}{3}$ f $\dfrac{3}{4}, \dfrac{2}{5}, \dfrac{1}{2}$

2 Work out the answers to these calculations. Write the answers as a fraction.

a $15 \div 7 =$ b $13 \div 4 =$ c $25 \div 6 =$

d $32 \div 5 =$ e $34 \div 9 =$ f $75 \div 8 =$

3 Work out these fraction multiplications.

a $12 \times \dfrac{1}{2} =$ b $24 \times \dfrac{1}{4} =$ c $18 \times \dfrac{1}{3} =$

d $32 \times \dfrac{1}{8} =$ e $20 \times \dfrac{1}{5} =$ f $49 \times \dfrac{1}{7} =$

 Solve each of these word problems. Show all your working out.

1 In a jar of sweets there are $\dfrac{4}{9}$ red sweets and $\dfrac{1}{3}$ purple sweets.

a Are there more red or purple sweets?

b The rest of the sweets are striped. What fraction of the jar is striped sweets?

c There are 28 red sweets. How many purple sweets are there?

d The shopkeeper decides to put the sweets into bags of nine. What fraction of the sweets will be in each bag? Write the division calculation to help him.

2 This jar of sweets has 108 sweets in it. The shopkeeper is writing some multiplication calculations to help him work out how many ways he could bag the sweets up.

a Finish his calculations.

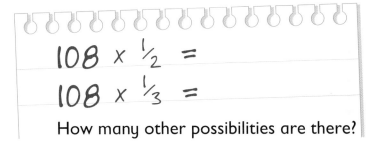

$108 \times \frac{1}{2} =$

$108 \times \frac{1}{3} =$

How many other possibilities are there?

b Before the shopkeeper can bag them up, seven friends come in and buy the whole jar. They decide to share the sweets equally. Write the division calculation. Write the quotient as a fraction.

c They give the left-over sweets to one person's younger sister. This friend says she will pay for these sweets. The whole jar costs £5.40. How much does each person have to pay? How much extra does the friend have to pay for her little sister's sweets?

Work with a partner. Make up a sweets problem for your partner to work out.

Think carefully about the number of sweets in the jar and the fractions you use.

You must know the answers yourself before you give the problem to your partner.

What's my partner?

 ❶ What is the decimal equivalent for these fractions? Try and remember these 'pairs'.

a  $\frac{1}{2}$ b  $\frac{1}{4}$ c $\frac{3}{4}$

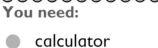

You need:
● calculator

d  $\frac{1}{5}$ e  $\frac{1}{10}$ f  $\frac{1}{100}$

❷ Work out the decimal equivalent for these fractions using a calculator.

a  $\frac{3}{5}$ b  $\frac{1}{8}$ c  $\frac{7}{10}$ d  $\frac{9}{20}$ e $\frac{18}{25}$

f  $\frac{6}{8}$ g $\frac{2}{5}$ h $\frac{3}{10}$ i  $\frac{7}{25}$ j  $\frac{3}{8}$

❶ Work out the decimal equivalent for these fractions. Use a calculator. Show your working.

You will need to round some decimals to 3 places.

You need:
● calculator

a  $\frac{3}{8}$ b $\frac{5}{9}$ c $\frac{6}{13}$

Example

$\frac{3}{14}$ $1 \div 14 = 0.0714285$
rounds to 0.071
$0.071 \times 3 = 0.214$

d $\frac{16}{20}$

e $\frac{1}{6}$

f $\frac{19}{25}$

g $\frac{2}{3}$

h $\frac{5}{6}$

i $\frac{3}{20}$

j $\frac{7}{15}$

k $\frac{3}{16}$

l $\frac{5}{14}$

2 Work out the **simplest** fraction equivalent for these decimals. Show your working.

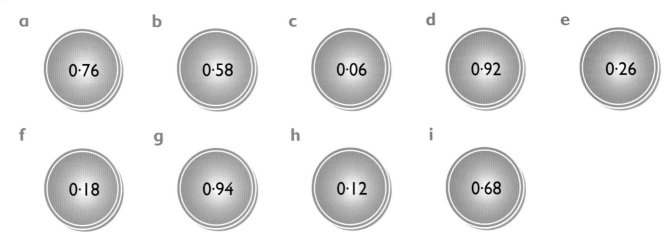

a 0·76

b 0·58

c 0·06

d 0·92

e 0·26

f 0·18

g 0·94

h 0·12

i 0·68

Work out the fraction and decimal equivalent for these percentages. Make sure the fraction is in its simplest form.

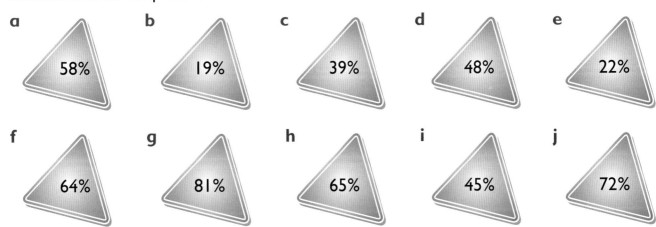

a 58%

b 19%

c 39%

d 48%

e 22%

f 64%

g 81%

h 65%

i 45%

j 72%

Convert and compare

● **Find equivalent decimals and fractions**

 Order the fractions, smaller to larger, by converting them to decimals. Use a calculator.

You need:
● calculator

a $\frac{4}{5}$ $\frac{2}{3}$

b $\frac{3}{8}$ $\frac{5}{20}$

c $\frac{96}{100}$ $\frac{9}{10}$

d $\frac{21}{25}$ $\frac{5}{8}$

e $\frac{1}{6}$ $\frac{2}{8}$

f $\frac{1}{3}$ $\frac{7}{20}$

g $\frac{68}{100}$ $\frac{3}{5}$

h $\frac{3}{4}$ $\frac{16}{20}$

i $\frac{3}{25}$ $\frac{1}{10}$

j $\frac{7}{8}$ $\frac{8}{10}$

k $\frac{2}{5}$ $\frac{8}{25}$

l $\frac{37}{100}$ $\frac{3}{10}$

 Order the fractions, smallest to largest, by converting them to decimals. Use a calculator.

You will need to round some decimals to 3 places.

You need:
● calculator

a $\frac{4}{7}$ $\frac{3}{11}$ $\frac{2}{5}$

d $\frac{7}{20}$ $\frac{1}{7}$ $\frac{5}{13}$

b $\frac{7}{12}$ $\frac{6}{15}$ $\frac{4}{9}$

e $\frac{6}{11}$ $\frac{9}{17}$ $\frac{3}{8}$

c $\frac{13}{18}$ $\frac{8}{12}$ $\frac{4}{5}$

f $\frac{18}{21}$ $\frac{7}{13}$ $\frac{4}{10}$

g $\dfrac{63}{100}$ $\dfrac{4}{9}$ $\dfrac{6}{15}$

m $\dfrac{12}{100}$ $\dfrac{1}{8}$ $\dfrac{1}{9}$

h $\dfrac{4}{14}$ $\dfrac{9}{24}$ $\dfrac{13}{34}$

n $\dfrac{3}{4}$ $\dfrac{6}{7}$ $\dfrac{11}{13}$

i $\dfrac{1}{2}$ $\dfrac{5}{8}$ $\dfrac{67}{100}$

o $\dfrac{1}{9}$ $\dfrac{3}{17}$ $\dfrac{4}{22}$

j $\dfrac{9}{17}$ $\dfrac{13}{24}$ $\dfrac{6}{9}$

p $\dfrac{28}{100}$ $\dfrac{8}{12}$ $\dfrac{9}{13}$

k $\dfrac{4}{7}$ $\dfrac{3}{8}$ $\dfrac{2}{9}$

q $\dfrac{9}{26}$ $\dfrac{3}{11}$ $\dfrac{33}{100}$

l $\dfrac{4}{16}$ $\dfrac{2}{11}$ $\dfrac{5}{21}$

r $\dfrac{4}{5}$ $\dfrac{12}{14}$ $\dfrac{19}{23}$

Copy these pyramids. Convert the fractions to decimals so that you can add them and complete the pyramid.
Add the two bricks together and write the total in the brick above.

a

$4\dfrac{3}{5}$ $2\dfrac{4}{7}$ $1\dfrac{9}{15}$ $5\dfrac{2}{9}$

b

6·92

$\dfrac{6}{8}$ $6\dfrac{2}{12}$ $5\dfrac{7}{17}$ $2\dfrac{9}{14}$

You need:
● calculator

99

Fractions, decimals and percentages

● **Find equivalent fractions, decimals and percentages**

 Copy and complete the table.
Use a calculator to work out
the missing decimals and percentages.

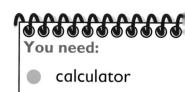

You need:
● calculator

	Fraction	Decimal	Percentage
a	$\frac{1}{2}$	$1 \div 2 = 0\cdot\boxed{}$	$100 \div 2 = \boxed{}$ %
b	$\frac{1}{4}$	$1 \div 4 = 0\cdot\boxed{}$	$100 \div 4 = \boxed{}$ %
c	$\frac{1}{5}$	$1 \div 5 = 0\cdot\boxed{}$	$100 \div 5 = \boxed{}$ %
d	$\frac{1}{3}$	$1 \div 3 = 0\cdot\boxed{}$	$100 \div 3 = \boxed{}$ %
e	$\frac{1}{8}$	$1 \div 8 = 0\cdot\boxed{}$	$100 \div 8 = \boxed{}$ %
f	$\frac{1}{10}$	$1 \div 10 = 0\cdot\boxed{}$	$100 \div 10 = \boxed{}$ %
g	$\frac{3}{4}$	$1 \div 4 = 0\cdot\boxed{} \times 3 = 0\cdot\boxed{}$	$100 \div 4 = \boxed{}$ % $\boxed{}$ % $\times 3 = \boxed{}$ %

① Copy and complete the following triangles.

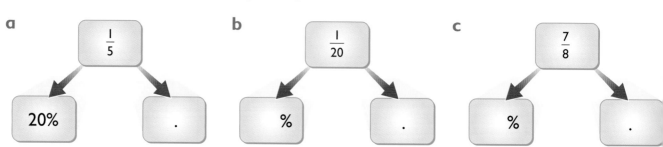

a $\frac{1}{5}$ 20%   .

b $\frac{1}{20}$ %   .

c $\frac{7}{8}$ %   .

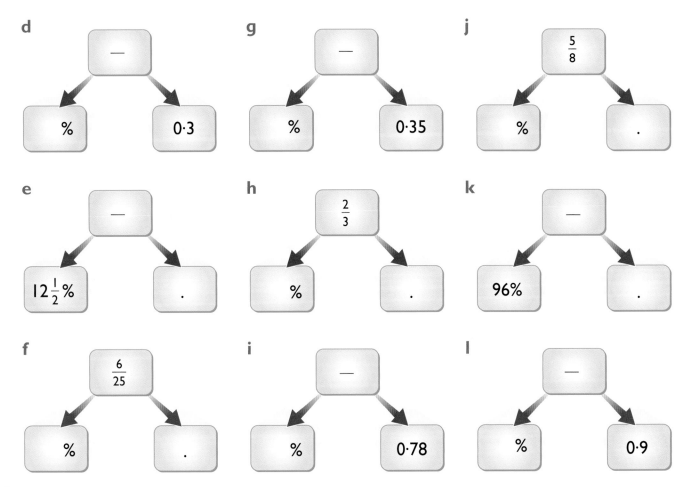

d

☐ — → ☐ %   ☐ 0·3

g

☐ — → ☐ %   ☐ 0·35

j

☐ $\frac{5}{8}$ → ☐ %   ☐ .

e

☐ — → $12\frac{1}{2}$ %   ☐ .

h

☐ $\frac{2}{3}$ → ☐ %   ☐ .

k

☐ — → 96 %   ☐ .

f

☐ $\frac{6}{25}$ → ☐ %   ☐ .

i

☐ — → ☐ %   ☐ 0·78

l

☐ — → ☐ %   ☐ 0·9

2 Now make up some of your own.

Fraction dice

A game for two players

- Take turns to roll the dice and make a fraction. It must not be a top heavy fraction, for example, 7 and 3 becomes $\frac{3}{7}$ not $\frac{7}{3}$.

- Convert your fraction to a decimal.

- Compare your decimal to your partner's.

- The larger decimal scores a point.

- Keep going until one player scores 10 points.

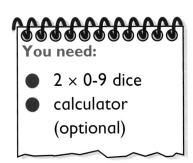

You need:

- 2 × 0-9 dice
- calculator (optional)

Percentage squares

 1 What fraction of each shape is shaded?

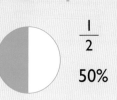

$\frac{1}{2}$

50%

a

b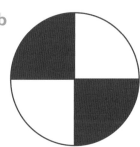

c

d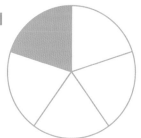

e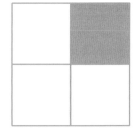

f

g

h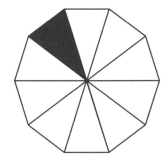

i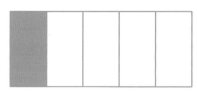

j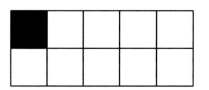

k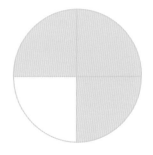

2 What percentage of each shape is shaded?

102

1 Work out the percentages of the amount of the number in the middle.
Record your calculations.

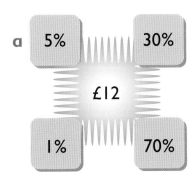

a 5% | 30% | £12 | 1% | 70%

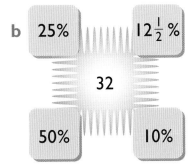

b 25% | 12½% | 32 | 50% | 10%

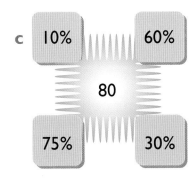

c 10% | 60% | 80 | 75% | 30%

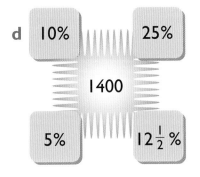

d 10% | 25% | 1400 | 5% | 12½%

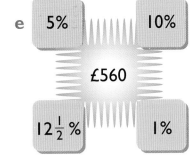

e 5% | 10% | £560 | 12½% | 1%

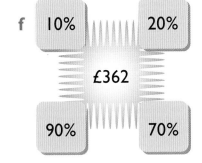

f 10% | 20% | £362 | 90% | 70%

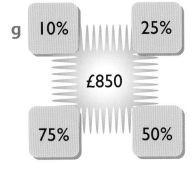

g 10% | 25% | £850 | 75% | 50%

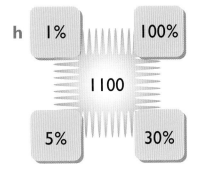

h 1% | 100% | 1100 | 5% | 30%

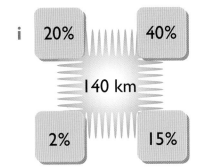

i 20% | 40% | 140 km | 2% | 15%

2 Choose 10 of your answers to write as fractions.

Complete each statement in as many ways as you can.

Example
4 is 50% of 8

1 4 is ☐ % of ☐   **2** 20 is ☐ % of ☐

3 15 is ☐ % of ☐   **4** 3·20 is ☐ % of ☐   **5** 4·32 is ☐ % of ☐

Concert hall problems

Solve problems involving fractions, decimals and percentages

Work out the answers to these word problems.

Choose the best method for each one.

Show all your working out.

> 300 people go to a show.
>
> Each ticket costs £2.20.
>
> Programmes cost 90p.

a What is the total of the ticket money collected?

b $\frac{1}{4}$ of the takings from the tickets was given to charity. How much was this?

c $\frac{4}{10}$ of the people who came arrived by bus. How many people was this?

d 75% of the audience bought a programme. How many people was this?

e How much money was made from the sale of programmes?

f If everyone had bought a programme, how much more money would have been made?

Work out the answers to these word problems.

Choose the best method for each one.

Show all your working out.

> 612 people go to a concert.
>
> Each ticket costs £2.90.
>
> Ice creams cost 80p.
>
> Programmes cost £1.30.

a What is the total of the ticket money collected?

b $\frac{4}{10}$ of the takings from the tickets was given to charity. How much was this?

c $\frac{1}{6}$ of the people who came bought an ice cream.
How much money was collected from this?

d 25% of the people who came bought a programme.
How much money was collected from this?

e 33% of the people bought an ice cream and a programme.
How much money was collected from this?

f At the beginning of the evening, the concert hall had 600 programmes.
Halfway through the evening they had sold 90% of them. How many had been sold
and how much money was taken?

g After the concert, the remaining programmes were reduced in price by 10%, and
half of them were sold. How much more money was taken?

At the end of a concert, this is how the money was used:

$\frac{1}{4}$ was given to charity.

$\frac{1}{8}$ had been spent on printing the programmes.

$\frac{3}{10}$ was used to pay all the staff.

There was £1326 left.

How much did they start with?

Vertically adding

● **Use efficient written methods to add whole numbers and decimals**

Addition facts to 20

1 Write the answers to these calculations as quickly as you can.

a 12 + 6	h 8 + 8	o 4 + 9
b 4 + 15	i 9 + 5	p 8 + 2
c 9 + 6	j 13 + 7	q 13 + 4
d 7 + 5	k 6 + 3	r 14 + 0
e 7 + 7	l 11 + 6	s 9 + 9
f 6 + 1	m 10 + 8	t 11 + 4
g 2 + 17	n 3 + 5	u 12 + 4

> You must learn all the addition facts to 20 by heart!

2 Copy out these calculations vertically and work out the answer. Remember to make an estimate first and to check your answer.

a 365 + 3921	i 7306 + 493
b 759 + 8541	j 351·8 + 632·7
c 5962 + 4198	k 6914·2 + 485·7
d 625 + 384	l 6849·26 + 584·21
e 725 + 4593	m 526·1 + 367·8
f 9607 + 831	n 1633·55 + 486·72
g 5333 + 6248	o 596·78 + 153·49
h 4930 + 483	p 664·95 + 725·88

1 Make up 10 addition calculations using these numbers. Remember to make an estimate first and to check your answer.

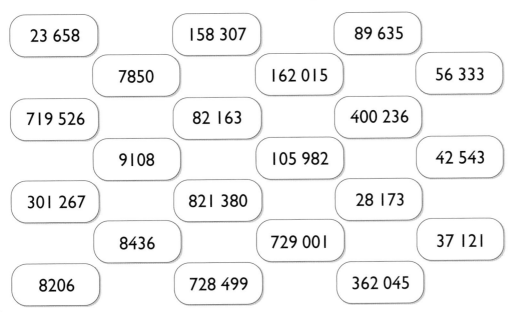

23 658

158 307

89 635

7850

162 015

56 333

719 526

82 163

400 236

9108

105 982

42 543

301 267

821 380

28 173

8436

729 001

37 121

8206

728 499

362 045

Example

```
   89 635
+  56 333
  145 968
     1
```

2 Make up 10 more addition calculations using these numbers. Remember to make an estimate first and to check your answer.

584·85

621·4

9601·7

548·33

704·9

6477·53

1588·614

826·901

76·591

847·006

152·92

9518·71

72·595

624·51

68·571

6914·35

8256.43

872·685

99·01

5421·52

4293·167

 Using the digits 2, 0, 7, 9, 4, 3 make these totals by adding two numbers together. In each calculation each digit can only be used once.

a 3·094   **b** 56·23   **c** 1013·2   **d** 51·73   **e** 950·2

Vertically subtracting

Use efficient written methods to subtract whole numbers and decimals

 Subtraction facts to 20

1 Write the answers to these calculations as quickly as you can.

a 15 – 6	h 13 – 8	o 12 – 7
b 9 – 5	i 9 – 9	p 18 – 9
c 17 – 11	j 18 – 13	q 20 – 12
d 12 – 8	k 14 – 11	r 19 – 18
e 19 – 9	l 16 – 3	s 5 – 0
f 10 – 6	m 16 – 7	t 15 – 7
g 20 – 5	n 8 – 3	u 19 – 6

You must learn all the subtraction facts to 20 by heart!

2 Copy out these calculations vertically and work out the answer. Remember to make an estimate first and to check your answer.

a 4835 – 1256	i 95 317 – 4526
b 842 – 351	j 782·3 – 51·9
c 7802 – 3657	k 485·12 – 96·43
d 19 873 – 523	l 455·9 – 122·4
e 14 932 – 7521	m 6933·5 – 42·8
f 6388 – 921	n 78·56 – 24·99
g 71 952 – 825	o 653·56 – 81·59
h 77 604 – 15 402	p 6214·87 – 591·06

1 Make up 10 subtraction calculations using these numbers. Remember to make an estimate first and to check your answer.

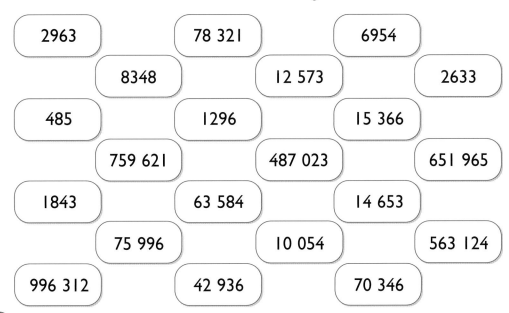

2963	78 321	6954
8348	12 573	2633
485	1296	15 366
759 621	487 023	651 965
1843	63 584	14 653
75 996	10 054	563 124
996 312	42 936	70 346

Example

5 12 1
2 6̸ 3̸ 3
−   485
_____
2 1 4 8

2 Make up 10 more subtraction calculations using these numbers. Remember to make an estimate first and to check your answer.

563·19	4852·3	4826·87
9603·54	2963·025	458·36
6972·156	3935·12	54 023·8
33·658	486·3	730·25
972·011	7523·15	45 986·12
54 632·8	9412·66	78 526·23
452 168·1	599 601·88	356·104

Using the digits 1, 2, 3, 4, 5, 6 make these totals by subtracting two numbers. In each calculation each digit can only be used once.

a 27·3   b 2·14   c 41·92   d 28·84   e 89·2   f 1·29

Ratio and proportion with shapes

● Solve simple problems involving ratio and proportion

Write the ratio and proportion for each of these patterns.

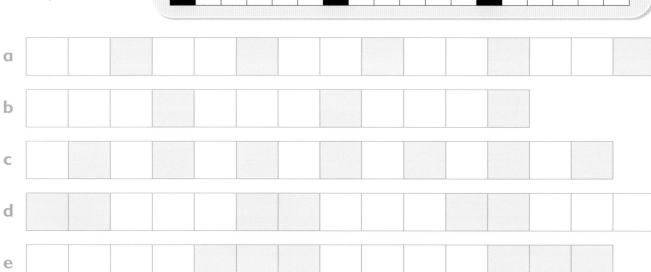

Example

The ratio of black squares to white squares is 1 to every 5.
The proportion of black squares to white squares is 1 in every 6.

a

b

c

d

e

Write the ratio and proportion for each of these patterns.

a

How many red and blue squares would there be if the pattern continued for 20 squares?

b

How many red and green apples would there be if the pattern continued for 35 apples?

c

How many yellow and orange stars would there be if the pattern continued for 63 stars?

d

How many happy and unhappy faces would there be if the pattern continued for 56 faces?

e

How many black and ginger cats would there be if the pattern continued for 72 cats?

What is the ratio of the distance around your head to your height?

Is the ratio the same for other people?

Do adults have the same ratio?

You need:
● measuring tape

111

Ratio and proportion

Solve simple problems involving ratio and proportion

1. I can swim 40 m for every 10 m my friend swims.

   a If I swim 160 m, how far will my friend swim?

   b If my friend swims 60 m, how far will I swim?

   c If we swim 300 m in total, how far will each of us have swum?

2. For every 2 days it rained last month, it was sunny for 3.

   a If it rained for 8 days, how many days was it sunny?

   b If it was sunny for 15 days, how many days did it rain?

   c Over 30 days, how many sunny days and how many rainy days were there?

3. For every 60p pocket money I get, I save 20p and spend 40p.

   a If I save 80p how much do I spend?

   b If I spend £2 how much do I save?

   c If I am given £6 pocket money, how much do I spend and how much do I save?

1. For every 2 pages of a book that Jill reads, Jack reads 6.

   a What is the ratio of pages read by Jill to the pages read by Jack?

   b What is the proportion of pages read by Jill?

   c What is the proportion of pages read by Jack?

   d If Jack reads 36 pages, how many will Jill have read?

   e If Jill reads 8 pages, how many will Jack have read?

2. Anne and Tony have made 28 cakes. Anne ate 8 of the cakes and Tony ate the rest.

   a What is the ratio of cakes eaten by Anne to cakes eaten by Tony?

   b What is the proportion of cakes eaten by Anne?

   c What is the proportion of cakes eaten by Tony?

   d When Anne had eaten 4 of the cakes, how many had Tony eaten?

   e When Tony had eaten 15 of the cakes, how many had Anne eaten?

3 In a box of chocolates, there are 3 plain chocolates to every 5 milk chocolates.

   a What is the ratio of plain chocolates to milk chocolates?

   b What is the proportion of plain chocolates?

   c What is the proportion of milk chocolates?

   d If there are 15 plain chocolates, what will be the total number of chocolates?

   e If there are 40 milk chocolates, what will be the total number of chocolates?

4 The recipe says that to make a sauce, you need $1\frac{1}{2}$ litres of water to every $\frac{1}{2}$ litre of milk.

   a What is the ratio of water to milk?

   b What is the proportion of water?

   c What is the proportion of milk?

   d If 10 litres of sauce are made, how much milk will be used?

   e If 4 litres of milk are used, how much sauce will be made?

1 I made 30 cakes and ate $\frac{1}{5}$ of them. My sister ate the rest.

   a What proportion of the cakes did I eat?

   b What proportion of the cakes did my sister eat?

   c What is the ratio of cakes eaten by me to cakes eaten by my sister?

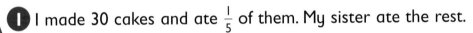

2 I saved 40% of my money. I have £12 saved.

   a What proportion of the money did I spend?

   b What proportion of the money did I save?

   c What is the ratio of money saved to money spent?

3 I had 24 sweets. I gave my brother 8 of them.

   a What proportion of the sweets did I have?

   b What proportion of the sweets did my brother have?

   c What is the ratio of my sweets to my brother's sweets?

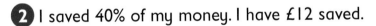

Holiday currencies

The Richards family are planning a holiday to Australia in July. There are two adults and three children aged 1 year, 8 years and 11 years. They need to purchase these things before they can travel.

Work out the total cost involved for the Richards family to fly to Australia.

Family travel insurance: £95

Air tickets

● Adults: £756
● Children under 12 years: £567
● Infants under 2 years: 25% of adult ticket price

Airport departure tax: £20 per person

Children under 2 years: half price

1 Use the information in the 'tourist rates' to find out how much of each of the currencies of the countries below you would receive when exchanging pounds.

Copy and complete the table.

To convert pounds (£) into other currencies, multiply the number of pounds by the exchange rate.

TOURIST RATES (June) £ =			
Australia ($)	2.38	New Zealand ($)	3.03
Canada ($)	2.15	Norway (krone)	12.62
Denmark (krone)	11.42	Saudi Arabia (riyal)	5.50
Hong Kong ($)	11.37	Singapore ($)	2.49
India (rupee)	60.65	South Africa (rand)	9.94
Israel (shekel)	5.75	Switzerland (franc)	2.39
Japan (yen)	156.96	Thailand (baht)	54.36
Malaysia (ringgit)	5.50	Turkey (lira)	900132
Mexico (peso)	13.67	USA ($)	1.46

Country	Currency	Exchange rate	Round to nearest whole number	£5	£10	£25	£50	£100
Australia								
India								
Norway								
Mexico								
Israel								
Japan								

2 While on holiday you buy some items. Use the exchange rates to work out the cost of each item in English pounds. (Round each currency rate to the nearest whole number.)

To convert other currencies into pounds, divide the amount by the exchange rate.

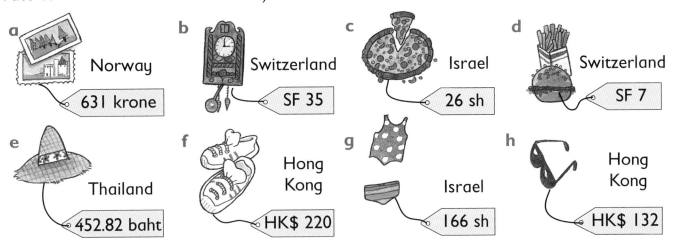

a Norway 631 krone

b Switzerland SF 35

c Israel 26 sh

d Switzerland SF 7

e Thailand 452.82 baht

f Hong Kong HK$ 220

g Israel 166 sh

h Hong Kong HK$ 132

Here are the 'tourist rates' at a different time of the year.

1 Choose 15 countries to visit. Work out if the exchange rate has increased (↑) or decreased (↓) between April and June, and by how much.

2 Work out the difference between exchanging £10 in April and June. Write how much, and if it has increased (↑) or decreased (↓).

3 Decide when the better time to travel to each country would be based on this information.

4 Copy and complete the table to record your information. An example has been done for you.

TOURIST RATES (April) £ =			
Australia ($)	2.57	New Zealand ($)	3.09
Canada ($)	2.25	Norway (krone)	13.61
Denmark (krone)	12.49	Saudi Arabia (riyal)	5.72
Hong Kong ($)	11.80	Singapore ($)	2.55
India (rupee)	61.55	South Africa (rand)	10.31
Israel (shekel)	5.84	Switzerland (franc)	2.63
Japan (yen)	165.21	Thailand (baht)	54.92
Malaysia (ringgit)	5.72	Turkey (lira)	930029
Mexico (peso)	13.42	USA ($)	1.52

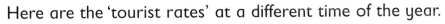

Country	Exchange rate		↑ or ↓	Difference between exchanging £10 in April or June	Best time to travel
	April	June			
USA	1·52	1·46	↓ 0·06	US $0·60	April

Travel problems

● **Choose and use appropriate number operations to solve problems involving money**

 Look at the Return Fares in the ● section. Don't forget the ones on the opposite page

1 List the destinations shown in the adverts in the order of cost, beginning with the cheapest

2 What is the difference in price between the cheapest flight and the most expensive flight

3 Calculate the cost of three adults travelling to:

    a Toronto   b Hong Kong   c Cape Town   d Auckland

4 Calculate the cost of six adults travelling to:

    a New York   b Singapore   c Nairobi   d Sydney

 Use the information on the flight adverts to answer the questions.

1 a How much would it cost to travel one way to each destination in the USA and Canada?

   b What is the difference in cost between return flights to New York and Los Angeles?

   c Work out how much the accommodation costs per night on the New York City Break.

USA Canada

Return Fares from London to	
New York	£184
Florida	£247
Toronto	£265
Los Angeles	£267

New York City Break
3 nights from **£367**
(accommodation + flight)

2 a How much more does it cost to fly to Singapore than Dubai?

   b Calculate the one way fare to each of these destinations.

   c How much does the accommodation cost per night on the holiday in Bangkok, Thailand?

Far East Middle East

Return Fares from London to	
Dubai	£255
Bangkok	£339
Hong Kong	£368
Singapore	£407

Thailand
8 nights from **£594**
(accommodation + flight)

3 a How much does the accomodation in Cape Town cost per night?

   b Breakfast and dinner is 25% of the accomodation cost per night. How much does it cost? How much for the room only?

Africa

Return Fares from London to	
Jo'burg	£296
Cape Town	£352
Nairobi	£354
Durban	£514

South Africa
5 nights from **£941**
(accommodation + flight)

4 a What is the difference in price between a return fare to Melbourne and a return to Sydney?

b Children under 12 pay 25% less than the adult fare. How much does it cost for a child to travel to each destination?

c How much for a family of two adults and two children to fly to Perth?

Australia
New Zealand

Return **Fares** from London to	
Sydney	£469
Auckland	£526
Perth	£560
Melbourne	£566

Australia
from **£538** Book by 30 June
(accommodation + flight)

Special: Round the World Fare £849.

Travel in the same direction. Take up to 1 year to complete.

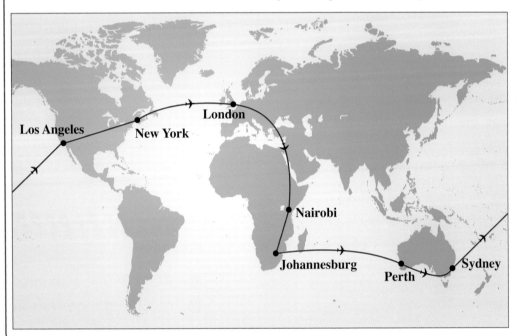

USA/CANADA return fares	
New York	£239
Boston	£239
Chicago	£239
Washington	£239
Los Angeles	£279
Las Vegas	£279
Miami	£269
Toronto	£265
Havana	£359
Mexico	£355

Worldwide return fares	
Sydney	£465
Perth	£548
Auckland	£547
Bangkok	£327
Hong Kong	£348
Dubai	£362
Jo'Burg	£324
Cape Town	£357
Nairobi	£377

1 What is the difference in cost between travelling to each destination shown on the map on a separate trip starting each time at London, and taking a Round the World Fare?

2 The Travel Shop is offering a 50% discount on all return flights. Which option is cheaper? By how much?

Reflecting flags

- Solve a problem in a systematic way
- Record the information in a problem or puzzle

You can make a flag with 1 blue and 8 yellow squares in three different ways.

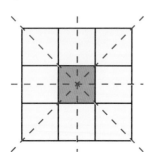 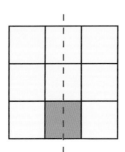 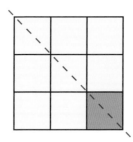

You need:

- RCM 8: 3 × 3 square grids
- colouring materials in blue, yellow and red

Rotations of the same design are not allowed.

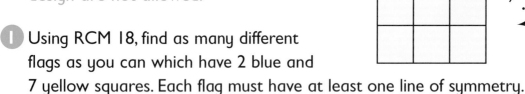

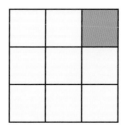 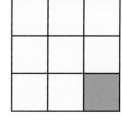

 1 Using RCM 18, find as many different flags as you can which have 2 blue and 7 yellow squares. Each flag must have at least one line of symmetry.

2 Mark the lines of symmetry in each flag with dotted red lines.

1 Using RCM 18, draw the different symmetrical flags which can be made with 3 blue squares and 6 yellow squares.

You need:

- RCM 8: 3 × 3 square grids
- colouring materials in blue, yellow and red

Remember

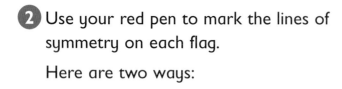

Rotations of the same design are not allowed.

2 Use your red pen to mark the lines of symmetry on each flag.

Here are two ways:

3 How many different flags can you make which have 4 blue squares and 5 yellow squares?

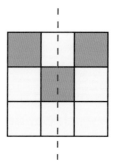 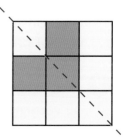

4 What if you have 5 blue squares and 4 yellow squares? How many different flags can you make?

5 Copy and complete the table below.

Number of blue squares	Number of flags
1	3
2	6
3	
4	
5	
6	
7	
8	

Three-colour flags

How many different four square flags can you make using only 3 colours?

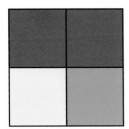 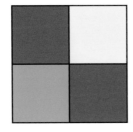 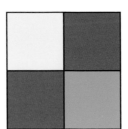

Can you think of a quick way to find all the possible combinations of colours?

You need:

● RCM 7: 2 × 2 square flags
● colouring materials in three different colours

HINT

● Begin with, say, 2 blue, 1 yellow and 1 green square and find all the different flags.

● Rotations of the same design **are** allowed.

Calculating numbers

1 To find the number in the square:

- multiply the top and bottom numbers;
- multiply the left and right numbers;
- find the difference between the numbers;
- write the answer in the square.

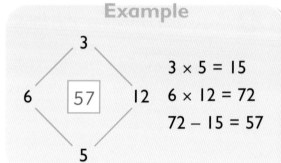

Example

3

6 [57] 12

5

$3 \times 5 = 15$
$6 \times 12 = 72$
$72 - 15 = 57$

a
6

8 ☐ 12

11

b
14

25 ☐ 15

21

c
23

13 ☐ 27

16

d
25

1·2 ☐ 9

0·6

2 Find the missing number in these squares.

a
8

11 19 9

☐

b
5

12 45 10

☐

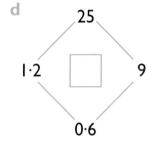

You need:
● calculator

1 Copy and complete.

a $9109 \times 1 =$
$9109 \times 2 =$
$9109 \times 3 =$
$9109 \times 4 =$
$9109 \times 5 =$

b $999·999 \times 2 =$
$999·999 \times 3 =$
$999·999 \times 4 =$
$999·999 \times 5 =$
$999·999 \times 6 =$

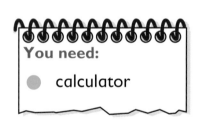

You need:
● calculator

2 Without using a calculator continue each calculation to:

a 9109 × 9 =   b 999·999 × 9 =

Check your answers using a calculator.

3 a Copy and complete.

12 345 679 × 9 =

12 345 679 × 18 =

12 345 679 × 27 =

12 345 679 × 36 =

b Write about any patterns you notice.

c Predict the answers to:

12 345 679 × 63 =

12 345 679 × 54 =

12 345 679 × 81 =

d Check your predictions.

4 Will this pattern continue to 5 rows?

Check.

Will it go on to 6 rows?

To 7 rows? Investigate.

$$1 + 2 = 3$$

$$4 + 5 + 6 = 7 + 8$$

$$9 + 10 + 11 + 12 = 13 + 14 + 15$$

$$16 + 17 + 18 + 19 + 20 =$$

End of the road

Begin with a 2-digit number.

Square each digit and add the answers.

Keep doing this until the answer is 1.

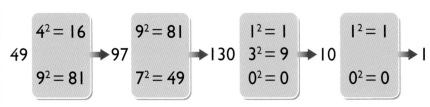

$49 \quad \begin{matrix} 4^2 = 16 \\ 9^2 = 81 \end{matrix} \rightarrow 97 \quad \begin{matrix} 9^2 = 81 \\ 7^2 = 49 \end{matrix} \rightarrow 130 \quad \begin{matrix} 1^2 = 1 \\ 3^2 = 9 \\ 0^2 = 0 \end{matrix} \rightarrow 10 \quad \begin{matrix} 1^2 = 1 \\ 0^2 = 0 \end{matrix} \rightarrow 1$

There are four 2-digit numbers between 10 and 30 where 1 is the end of the road. True or false? Investigate.

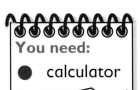

You need:
● calculator

Investigating squares

Record in a table the steps needed to solve a problem

a Copy these squares on to 1 cm squared paper.

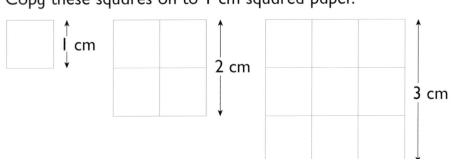

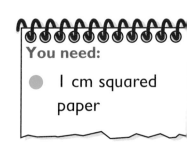

You need:

● 1 cm squared paper

b Draw the next square in the sequence.

c Copy and complete the table for the number of squares.

Length of side of square	Number of squares				
	1 × 1 sq	2 × 2 sq	3 × 3 sq	4 × 4 sq	5 × 5 sq
1 cm	1	0	0		
2 cm	4	1	0		
3 cm	9	4	1		
4 cm					
5 cm					

d Find the number of different sized squares that fit in a square with length of sides of 5 cm. Record your answers in the table.

1 Theo bought 12 square tiles for his bathroom.

He fixed them in 2 rows of 6 tiles above the wash basin.

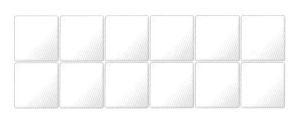

You need:

● 1 cm squared paper

He stood back to admire his work and said: 'I can see 17 squares altogether.'

Is he correct? Investigate.

Make a table like this to record your results.

Size of tiling	Number of tiles		
	single tiles	4 tiles	Total
2 × 1	2	0	2
2 × 2	4		
2 × 3	6		
2 × 4			
2 × 5			
2 × 6			

2 The next weekend he bought 18 square tiles for his kitchen. He fixed them to the wall above the kitchen sink in 3 rows of 6 tiles.

How many squares could he see altogether?

a Make a 3 × 3 × 3 cube with interlocking cubes.

Now imagine all the outside faces painted red.

b Find how many of the 1 cm cubes have:

0 red faces

1 red face

2 red faces

3 red faces.

c Do the same for a 4 × 4 × 4 cube and a 5 × 5 × 5 cube.

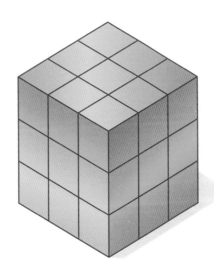

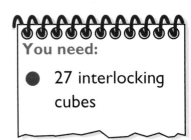

You need:

● 27 interlocking cubes

Maths Facts

Problem solving

The seven steps to problem solving

1 Read the problem carefully. **2** What do you have to find?

3 What facts are given? **4** Which of the facts do you need?

5 Make a plan. **6** Carry out your plan to obtain your answer. **7** Check your answer.

Number

Positive and negative numbers

```
–10  –9  –8  –7  –6  –5  –4  –3  –2  –1   0   1   2   3   4   5   6   7   8   9   10
```

Place value

1000	2000	3000	4000	5000	6000	7000	8000	9000
100	200	300	400	500	600	700	800	900
10	20	30	40	50	60	70	80	90
1	2	3	4	5	6	7	8	9
0·1	0·2	0·3	0·4	0·5	0·6	0·7	0·8	0·9
0·01	0·02	0·03	0·04	0·05	0·06	0·07	0·08	0·09
0·001	0·002	0·003	0·004	0·005	0·006	0·007	0·008	0·009

Fractions, decimals and percentages

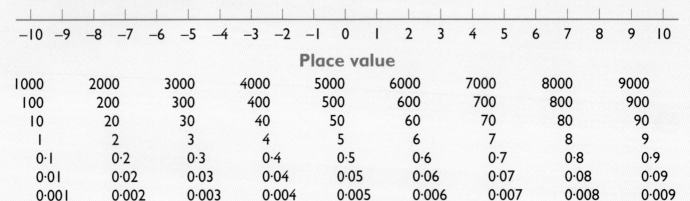

$\frac{1}{100} = 0·01 = 1\%$ $\qquad \frac{2}{100} = \frac{1}{50} = 0·02 = 2\%$ $\qquad \frac{5}{100} = \frac{1}{20} = 0·05 = 5\%$

$\frac{10}{100} = \frac{1}{10} = 0·1 = 10\%$ $\qquad \frac{1}{8} = 0·125 = 12·5\%$ $\qquad \frac{20}{100} = \frac{1}{5} = 0·2 = 20\%$

$\frac{25}{100} = \frac{1}{4} = 0·25 = 25\%$ $\qquad \frac{1}{3} = 0·333 = 33\frac{1}{3}\%$ $\qquad \frac{50}{100} = \frac{1}{2} = 0·5 = 50\%$

$\frac{2}{3} = 0·667 = 66\frac{2}{3}\%$ $\qquad \frac{75}{100} = \frac{3}{4} = 0·75 = 75\%$ $\qquad \frac{100}{100} = 1 = 100\%$

Number facts

Multiplication and division facts

	×1	×2	×3	×4	×5	×6	×7	×8	×9	×10
×1	1	2	3	4	5	6	7	8	9	10
×2	2	4	6	8	10	12	14	16	18	20
×3	3	6	9	12	15	18	21	24	27	30
×4	4	8	12	16	20	24	28	32	36	40
×5	5	10	15	20	25	30	35	40	45	50
×6	6	12	18	24	30	36	42	48	54	60
×7	7	14	21	28	35	42	49	56	63	70
×8	8	16	24	32	40	48	56	64	72	80
×9	9	18	27	36	45	54	63	72	81	90
×10	10	20	30	40	50	60	70	80	90	100

Tests of divisibility

2 The last digit is 0, 2, 4, 6 or 8.

3 The sum of the digits is divisible by 3.

4 The last two digits are divisible by 4.

5 The last digit is 5 or 0.

6 It is divisible by both 2 and 3.

7 Check a known near multiple of 7.

8 Half of it is divisible by 4 *or*
The last 3 digits are divisible by 8.

9 The sum of the digits is divisible by 9.

10 The last digit is 0.

Calculations

Addition

Whole numbers
Example: 6845 + 5758

```
  6845            6845
+ 5758          + 5758
 11 000          12 603
  1 500           ¹ ¹ ¹
    90
    13
 12 603
   ¹
```

Decimals
Example: 26.48 + 5.375

```
  26.48          26.48
+ 5.375        + 5.375
 20.000         31.855
 11.000          ¹ ¹
  0.700
  0.150
  0.005
 31.855
```

Subtraction

Whole numbers
Example: 7845 − 2367

```
 7845      or        700   130   15
−2367                700   140    5
   33 → 2400      7000 + 800 + 40 + 5
 5445 → 7845     − 2000 + 300 + 60 + 7
 5478              5000 + 400 + 70 + 8
```

```
       7 13 15
   7̶8̶4̶5̶
 − 2367
   5478
```

Decimals
Example: 639.35 − 214.46

```
 639.35    or            8 12 15
−214.46              6̶3̶9̶.̶3̶5̶
  00.54 → 215        −214.46
 424.35 → 639.35      424.89
 424.89
```

Multiplication

Whole numbers
Example: 5697 × 8

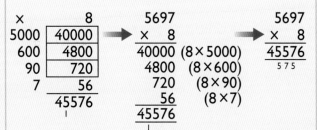

```
 ×  |   8          5697            5697
5000| 40000      ×    8          ×    8
600 |  4800       40000 (8×5000)  45576
 90 |   720        4800 (8×600)    ⁵⁷⁵
  7 |    56         720 (8×90)
     45576           56 (8×7)
       ¹           45576
                     ¹
```

Decimals
Example: 865.56 × 7

```
  ×   |   7          865.56                865.56
 800  | 5600       ×      7               ×      7
  60  |  420        5600   (7×800)         6058.92
   5  |   35         420   (7× 60)           ⁴ ³ ³ ⁴
 0.50 |  3.5          35   (7×  5)
 0.06 | 0.42          3.5  (7× 0.50)
      6058.92         0.42 (7× 0.06)
         ¹          6058.92
                       ¹
```

Whole numbers
Example: 364 × 87

```
  ×  |  80  |   7               364                   364
 300 |24000 | 2100    26100   ×  87                 ×  87
  60 | 4800 |  420     5220    24000  (300×80)       29120   364 × 80
   4 |  320 |   28      348     4800  (60×80)         2548   364 ×  7
                      31668      320  (4×80)         31668
                        ¹       2100  (300× 7)         ¹
                                 420  (60× 7)
                                  28  (4×  7)
                               31668
                                 ¹ ¹
```

Calculations

Division

Whole numbers

Example: 337 ÷ 8

```
8) 337
 -  80   (8 × 10)
   257
 -  80   (8 × 10)
   177
 -  80   (8 × 10)
    97
 -  80   (8 × 10)
    17
 -  16   (8 ×  2)
     1        42
```

Answer   42 R 1

➤

```
8) 337
 - 320   (8 × 40)
    17
 -  16   (8 ×  2)
     1        42
```

Answer   42 R 1

➤

```
      42  R 1
8) 337
   32
   17
   16
    1
```

➤

```
      42  R 1
8) 337
```

Decimals

Example: 78.3 ÷ 9

```
9) 78.3
 - 72.0   (9 × 8)
    6.3
 -  6.3   (9 × 0.7)
      0       8.7)
```

Answer   8.7

Example: 48.6 ÷ 3

```
3) 48.6
 - 30.0   (3 × 10)
   18.6
 - 18.0   (3 ×  6)
    0.6
 -  0.6   (3 ×  0.2)
      0       16.2
```

Answer   16.2

Order of operations

Brackets ➡ Division ➡ Multiplication ➡ Addition ➡ Subtraction

Shape and space

2–D shapes

 circle

 semi-circle

 right-angled triangle

 equilateral triangle

 isosceles triangle

 scalene triangle

 square

 rectangle

 rhombus

 kite

 parallelogram

 trapezium

 pentagon

 hexagon

heptagon

octagon

Shape and space

3–D solids

 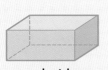 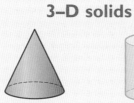

| cube | cuboid | cone | cylinder | sphere | hemi-sphere |

triangular prism | triangular-based pyramid (tetrahedron) | square-based pyramid | octahedron | dodecahedron

Co-ordinates

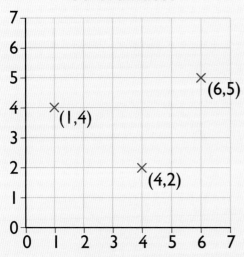

Reflection

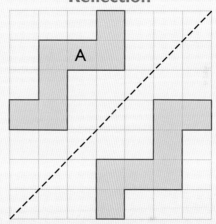

Shape A has been reflected along the diagonal line of symmetry

Rotation

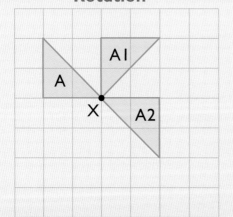

Shape A has been rotated through 90° (Shape A1) and 180° (Shape A2) around Point X

Translation

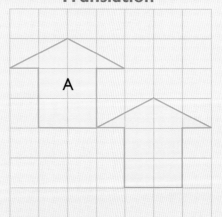

Shape A has been translated 3 squares to the right and 2 squares down.

Shape and space

Angles

Acute angle < 90°
Obtuse angle > 90° and < 180°
Reflex angle > 180° and < 360°
4 right angles (complete turn) = 360°

Right angle = 90°
Straight angle = 180°

Lines

Parallel lines

Perpendicular lines

Measures

Length

1 km	=	1000 m	=	100 000 cm	
0·1 km	=	100 m	=	10 000 cm	= 100 000 mm
0·01 km	=	10 m	=	1000 cm	= 10 000 mm
1 m	=	100 cm	=	1000 mm	
0·1 m	=	10 cm	=	100 mm	
0·01 m	=	1 cm	=	10 mm	
1 cm	=	10 mm		0·1 cm	= 1 mm

Mass

1 t	=	1000 kg	1 kg	= 1000 g
0.1 kg	=	100 g	0.01 kg	= 10 g

Capacity

1 litre	=	1000 ml	0.1 l	= 100 ml
0.01 l	=	10 ml	1 cl	= 10 ml

Metric units and imperial units

Length
8 km ≈ 5 miles (1 mile ≈ 1.6 km)

Mass
1 kg ≈ 2.2 lb
30 g ≈ 1 oz

Capacity
1 litre ≈ $1\frac{3}{4}$ pints
4.5 litres ≈ 8 pints (1 gallon)

Time

1 millennium	=	1000 years
1 century	=	100 years
1 decade	=	10 years
1 year	=	12 months
	=	365 days
	=	366 days (leap year)
1 week (wk)	=	7 days
1 day	=	24 hours
1 minute (min)	=	60 seconds

24 hour time

Perimeter and Area

P = perimeter   A = area   l = length   b = breadth

Perimeter of a rectangle:
P = 2l + 2b *or* P = 2 x (l + b)

Perimeter of a square:
P = 4 x l

Area of a rectangle:
A = l x b

Handling data

Planning an investigation

❶ Describe your investigation. ❷ Do you have a prediction? ❸ Describe the data you need to collect.
❹ How will you record and organise the data? ❺ What diagrams will you use to illustrate the data?
❻ What statistics will you calculate? ❼ How will you analyse the data and come to a conclusion?
❽ When you have finished, describe how your investigation could be improved.

Mode
The value that occurs most often.

Range
Difference between the largest value and the smallest value.

Median
Middle value when all the values have been ordered smallest to largest.

Mean
Total of all the values divided by the number of values.